Need To Read SERIES

Help for Home and Family

DR. JAMES DOBSON

Tyndale House Publishers, Inc.

WHEATON, ILLINOIS

Front cover photos: family, Robert Cushman Hayes;
father and son, Robert Cushman Hayes; grand-
mother and granddaughter, Molly Dean

Scripture quotations are taken from *The Simplified
Living Bible,* copyright © 1990 by KNT Charitable
Trust. All rights reserved.

Adapted for the Need to Read Series from *Dr. Dobson Answers Your Questions* © 1982 by Dr. James C.
Dobson. Used by permission.

ISBN 0-8423-318-4
Library of Congress Catalog Card Number: 90-71153
Copyright © 1990 by Tyndale House Publishers, Inc.
All rights reserved

Printed in the United States of America

96 95 94 93 92 91
 6   5   4   3   2   1

CONTENTS

INTRODUCTION

A few years ago my family took a vacation. We went with some friends. For three days we rode in rafts down the Rogue River in Oregon. One day I fell into the water. I thought I was going to die. At last one of my friends helped me. He pulled me into the big raft. Now I know what it feels like to nearly drown.

Now I often get letters from people. Others come to see me to talk of their problems. They often use the word "drown." That is how they feel. Some don't know what to do. They want answers.

Many of them have problems with their families. Some of them find help. Others learn to help themselves. I want to be like my friend. He pulled me out of the water when I was about to drown. That is what I want to do. I would like to help those with family problems. That is what this book is about. It is filled with questions. I have been asked these many times. Maybe some of the answers will help you.

CHAPTER 1

Life in the Family

I'm afraid I am not ready to raise my baby. He was born last month. I know how to feed and bathe him. But I am not sure about the future. How should I relate to him? What should I look for? What should I do these next four years?

Your question makes me think of a friend. He was flying a small plane. It was late in the day. Just as it got dark he tried to land. By then he could not see the runway. He flew around and around. He knew he would soon run out of gas. Someone heard his plane flying around. The person knew the plane was in trouble. The man drove to the runway. He drove his car across the runway. He shined his car lights so the pilot could see. The pilot then saw where he could land. The man had marked the borders of the runway.

We need borders in parenting. We need to know what we should and should not do. These borders need to be clear to us. Then parents can steer the family ship. Let me give you two truths. A child should know these during his first four years. He must be sure you mean them.

1. "I love you. You don't know how much I love you. You are precious to me. I thank God every day for you. I thank him that he let me raise you."
2. "Because I love you, I must teach you to obey me. That is the only way I can take care of you. I must protect you from things that might hurt you. The Bible says, 'Children, obey your parents. This is the right thing to do' (Eph. 6:1)."

This is a short answer. But the question you asked is crucial. I hope it gives you a place to begin. You must form your own plan of how to be a good parent.

Should parents force a child to eat?

I am no expert on feeding children. But I believe a child knows when he needs to eat. He knows how much he should eat. He knows when he is hungry. But parents should be careful what he eats. He should get the food his body needs. You could give him sugar. But then he wouldn't want to eat his next meal. He might sit at the table and just drink juice. Or he may just eat one kind of food. You may need to give him just one kind of food at a time. Begin with meat that is rich in iron. Or serve some other protein. Then you can give the child some other items. Then he has had the kinds of food he needs. After that he may not want to eat. You should not force him after that.

Appetites change as a child grows. When he is two or three years old, he won't eat very much. He has

stopped growing for a while. Later he will grow
more. Then he will eat more.

Someone said, "Children should be seen and not heard." What do you think of that?

People who say that know nothing about children.
It shows they don't know what a child needs. No
parent who loves his child believes that. Children are
like clocks. They must be allowed to run.

What if you have been in the wrong? Would you tell your child that you are sorry?

Yes, I would. And I have. A few years ago I was
very busy. I was tired and grumpy. One evening I was
very cross with my ten-year-old daughter. But I was
not being fair. I blamed her for things. They were not
her fault. She felt hurt a couple of times. There was no
need to upset her as I did. The next morning I felt
better. I had a good night's rest. Before she left for
school I talked to her. I said, "You know daddies are
not perfect. We get tired and grumpy just like other
people. We do things we are not proud of. I know I
wasn't fair with you last night. I was very grouchy. I
want you to forgive me."

She put her arms around me. She shocked me by
what she said. "I knew you were going to tell me you
were sorry. And it's OK. I forgive you."

Children know the struggles we go through. Sometimes they are more aware than we are.

I don't like the way my four-year-old is growing up. At the rate he is going, he will be a failure as an adult. Is there any way to tell what a child will be like when he grows up? Can I tell at this age what he will grow up to be?

I doubt it. Rene Voeltzel said, "We must not look too soon in a child for what he will later become." It is not fair to judge him so soon. Be patient. Give your little boy time to grow up. Be gentle with him. Work on the traits that concern you the most. But let him be a child. He will be little for such a short time!

Should I punish my son for wetting the bed?

It is never right to punish a child for what he doesn't want to do. It will make things worse. Other problems will result.

But is he doing it on purpose? He may be awake when he does it. If so, that is not the same. He may lie there and wet the bed because he is too lazy to get up. Then I would punish him. But most bed-wetting is not done on purpose.

We don't have enough money to take our family on long car trips. We can't pay for things like skiing. Can you tell us some simple things to do that our small kids will enjoy thinking about when they are older?

You don't have to spend a lot of money on good family life. Children love to do the same things over

and over. They enjoy hearing the same good story
many times. They laugh at the same silly jokes. You
may be ready to climb the wall because you have
heard them so often. You can make fun times out of
chores. But you must put some thought into it. They
should be moments of warmth and closeness. The key
is doing them over and over again. That gives them
things to remember.

Here is how we did it. When my family was
younger, I would put the kids to bed. As often as I
could I would help them. By that time of night, my
wife was very tired. She was glad for that help. It also
allowed me a few minutes or so with the kids. I may
have had a very busy day. But that was my time with
them.

I had to put a diaper on my son. It was hard to do
this to a squirming toddler. I thought I might as well
turn it into a fun time for both of us. So we played a
little game. I would talk to the diaper pins. I would say,
"Pins, don't stick him. I really don't think you should
stick him. See, he's being still. He's not wiggling
around. Tonight you don't have to stick him. Maybe
some other night. But don't stick him tonight."

My son loved the little game. He would listen
quietly. He would laugh. And his eyes got very big.
Sometimes he wiggled too much. I couldn't get the
diaper on him. Then I would touch the pin to his leg.
It was not enough to hurt him. He would say, "That
mean old pin sticked me, Daddy!" Every night he

would say, "Talk to the pins, Daddy." It was something we did with each other. Things like that became a fun time for both of us.

One man told me about his children who are now grown. He asked them about the time when they were growing up. Did they remember the vacations? What about the parks they saw? What did they remember? Their answer surprised him. What they enjoyed most was the times they had played with each other. They told him about the times he had gotten down on the floor and fought with them.

My daughter was the same way. She would rather tussle with me than go to Disneyland or the zoo. After we had had a tussle, I was very tired. She always thanked me for fighting with her. For some reason, kids love that kind of play. (Mothers hate it!) It is a simple way to show love. It doesn't occur in any other way.

I also like the idea of having one night a week together. We read to each other during this time. That might be hard to do when kids are not the same ages. I think it is a good idea. You can read *Tom Sawyer* and other books that have been loved through the ages. The idea is to do things together.

We are having more and more problems with money. What could you suggest?

Many books have been written about money problems. They are often caused by the same thing.

Many people want to have more and more things. We buy too many things we can't afford.

I have had many of the nice things of life. I have had new cars. I own a nice home. I have many things that save me time. I can tell you one thing. These things don't make me as happy as people said they would. I have found a very wise statement: "That which you own will one day own you." How true that is. I may buy something nice. Then I have to keep it fixed. I have to take care of it. It was supposed to give me pleasure. Now I have to take care of it. I have to oil it. I have to mow it. I have to clean it. Then I have to call someone to haul it away when it wears out. I could have spent that money on my family. I wasted a lot of time I could have spent with my children.

What have you bought in the last year that was a waste of money? It may have been a can opener. It now sits in the garage. It may have been a suit of clothes. You never wear it now. That thing was not bought with money. It was bought with time. You spent time to earn the money. You gave up some of your time for a piece of junk. I hate to be controlled by things.

I went to England not long ago. While there I saw many old castles. They are empty now. The men who built them are gone. These castles are all that remain to remind us of them.

I want to leave more than empty castles when I die. I know that my life is slipping away. Now is the best time to think about my life. I must use my time and efforts in the best way I can. I will soon reach the end of my days. I want to look back on something of real value. It must be more than houses and lands. I want to remember a lovely family. I want to think that I used my time well to help people. Nothing else makes much sense.

My kids fight a lot. They are jealous. How can I help them?

Help them not to compare themselves with each other. Their feelings are hurt when they do. We don't ask, "How am I doing?" We ask, "How am I doing compared to John?" We don't ask how fast we can run. We ask who finished first. Kids look at how well other kids do. They want to do better. So parents should try to keep their kids from comparing themselves with each other.

Children's feelings are easy to hurt. They worry about their looks. It hurts them to hear something nice about someone else. For example, Joan and Mary are sisters. Mother might say, "Joan is going to be a good-looking girl." Mary hears it. She feels hurt. From then on Mary will compete with Joan. She will say, "Yeah, I'm the ugly one." She already thought she was. Then she heard what mother said. Now she believes she is ugly.

Looks are important to kids today. It affects their self-esteem a lot. Be careful what you say around your children. Don't talk about how other children look. Your children may end up hating each other.

Some children are smarter than others. Be careful how you talk to your kids about brothers and sisters. Don't say, "Bill is smarter than Joe." Adults don't seem to know how much that hurts a child's feelings.

How well a child does in sports can also be a cause for trouble. It is hard to be "second best." This is true mostly for boys. Parents need to help their kids not to compare their skills with others.

CHAPTER 2

Spiritual Training of Children

How do I teach my child about God?

A child learns about God from his parents. Most people agree with that. A child at first obeys his parents. He trusts in them. Then he thinks God is like them. A parent might not like this fact. But it is still true.

Parents must accept that role. We must teach our children two things about God. First, God is a God of love. There are no limits to his love. Our children must come to know that. We must show them that God has mercy. He is tender to those he loves. We show this to them by the way we treat them. We should be loving. Then they will think God is loving. We should be kind and tender. Then they will think God is that way. But we must not forget. God is also someone we must obey. He ordered the whole world. He has warned us that he hates sin. "Sin makes us die," the Bible says (Rom. 6:23). We must show our children how to obey God. We do that by teaching them to obey us.

What years count most in teaching a child about God?

I think the fifth and sixth years are the most important. Before that, the child believes in God. That is because you do. At about age five or six, he comes to a fork in the road. He will begin to believe in God on his own. Or he may doubt that there is a God. But you should not wait until then. Start teaching about God now. Later years are important also. But the early years are very important.

My child is four years old. She comes home often in tears. She has been hit by one of her friends. I have taught her not to fight. I tell her it is wrong to hit others. But now her friends make it hard for her. What should I tell her? Should she fight back?

You are wise to teach your child not to hit or hurt others. But self-defense is not the same thing. Children do not want to share. They want the best toys. They make up their own rules. If they can get away with something, they do. I know some Christians may not like what I say. But I believe children should learn to defend themselves. The Bible says to turn the other cheek. But children can learn that later.

I once talked to a mother. She was worried about her daughter, Ann. The little girl's friend Joan would often hit her. One day the two were playing. Joan again hit Ann. Ann turned and smacked her back. The mother heard a loud cry. She looked out and saw Joan crying. Joan turned and went home. Ann came in the house. She said to her mother, "Joan socked me. So I had to help her not to hit me again." After that the two girls didn't fight.

Do you think we should let young children age five to ten listen to rock music on the radio?

No. Rock music is a part of adolescent culture. The words of these songs deal with dating. They are about romance, drugs, and the wrong kinds of love. You don't want your kids who are seven years old to hear that. At that age they should think of other things. Other things should excite them. Good fun for them would be camping, fishing, sports, and games.

But don't be too strict. Don't just force your child to stop. Try to get him involved with other things. That way he won't need to dream of the days to come.

I am trying to raise and train two boys. I have no husband to help me. I don't think I am doing a good job. Shouldn't the church try to help me?

Yes. That is one thing the church should do. Single parents need help. Jesus gave a clear command. He said we were to help and support those who have needs. He said, "You did these things for these my brothers. And in helping them, you were serving me!" (Matt. 25:40). I know Jesus meant those words. If so, then we should help those without fathers or mothers. If we do so, we are doing it for God. The Bible says one who is "pure and without fault" takes care of orphans and widows (Jas. 1:27). We will have to appear before God one day. We will answer for the way we helped those in need. Men in the church should care for boys without fathers. They should do boy-type things with them. They should play ball and toss Frisbees together. They should help the young mother with heavy jobs. They should do repair jobs. They might put a new roof on a house. They could paint her house. She may also need money when the kids are small. The Bible is clear. If there is a need, Christians should meet it.

We have heard a lot about toy guns. Do you think that children should play with them?

Kids have played cowboys and Indians for years. Children love to play combat games. I think people worry too much about that. Young boys live in a woman's world. They are around Mother all day. Their teachers are most often women. It is a sugar-and-spice world for them. I think it is healthy for boys to think of male models. At times these will be combat games. Boys have fun saying, "Bang! Bang! You're dead!"

But you should take care. I would not let kids watch too much shooting and killing on television. The movies and television have a big effect on kids. It is not good for them to get too excited over killing and shooting. If they see too much, it could hurt them.

My husband and I are upset. We think our teenage daughter is turning away from her Christian beliefs. She was saved at an early age. She used to show a real love for the Lord. I tend to panic over things like this. Can you help me?

A small child accepts what he is told. He picks up his parents' beliefs. That is how it should be. God expects parents to guide their children. But someday the child must think for himself. He will look at all that he has been taught. He may accept what parents have taught him. Or the child may choose to turn away from his parents' views. The child must take this step someday. He must go from "what I've been told" to "what I believe." It is a major step in growing up.

Most teenagers start to question things they have been taught. They want to know if they are true. They may ask, "Is there really a God? Does he know me? Do I accept my parent's values? Are they right for me? Do I want what my parents want for my life?" These questions may go on for years.

These will be hard years for parents. Parents should know that this process is normal. It will hurt less if parents know it is coming. It is part of growing up.

At what age should I let my child decide about church and his beliefs in God?

About age sixteen, some kids don't want to be told what to believe. They don't want church forced down their throats. You should let them have some choice in what they believe. But if you exposed them to church in the right way, they will be more steady in their beliefs. The early years are the key. These years decide how they will believe when they are grown.

Parents should take a soft approach in spiritual things. But they should hold to some rules. Kids should be required to go to church. Until they are seventeen, they should keep that rule. I would say, "As long as you are under this roof, we will go to church. I can't tell you what to think. That is up to you. But I must do what God wants me to do. I promised him I would honor him in this home. That includes going to church."

CHAPTER 3

Discipline of the Very Young

Should I ever discipline a child under six months of age? How could I punish him? What would be right?

You don't need to punish a child under seven months of age. No matter what he does, it won't help. A child may try to wiggle when you diaper him. Many people will hit a child for that. That is not right. At that age a child will not know why you hit him. At that age he needs to be held. He needs love. He needs to hear a soothing voice. Feed him when he is hungry. Keep him clean, dry, and warm. These months are the base for his emotional growth. He should feel human warmth. He should know he is secure and loved.

My baby is eight months old. She is fussy and cries a lot. My doctor says she is all right. He says she cries to get me to pick her up. She wants to sit on my lap all day long. How can I make her stop fussing?

Babies can't talk, so they cry. They may be hungry. They may feel bad or tired. Their diaper may be wet.

So listen to their cries. They may be calls for help. But your doctor may be right. If you run each time your child cries, you may make the baby fussy. Even at that age, babies can learn to control their parents.

Give your baby all the care she needs. But do not come each time she cries. It will help her lungs if she cries some. But listen for the tone of her voice. A mother can tell if the baby has a serious need.

Should I discipline a child who is one year old?

A small child may try to find out who is boss. At seven months old this may start. These times will be few before he is one year old. But by that time, a parent can see what is ahead. My daughter began to try out her mother when she was nine months old. My wife was waxing the kitchen floor. The baby crawled to the edge of the floor. By then she knew what "No" meant. Still she crawled on the floor. My wife picked her up. She set her down in the doorway. Again she said, "No." The little girl crawled back onto the floor. My wife took her back. She said, "No" again. Seven times they did this. Then the baby began to cry. She gave up. She didn't come onto the floor again. That was the first time she tried to see who was boss.

How do you discipline a child who is one year old? Be very gentle. A child at this age is easy to control. No need to jerk a wristwatch from his hands. Show him a brightly colored object. Then take the

watch before he drops it. When you need to do so,
be firm. My daughter wanted to crawl on the waxed
floor. My wife had to be firm with her. Do not be
afraid of your child's tears. The baby soon knows that
tears can be used as a weapon. Have the courage to
lead your child. But don't be mean or gruff. These are
still the easy years. It will get harder when the child
grows older.

At what age can I expect my child to be quiet in church?

It takes self-control for a child to be quiet. It comes
slowly for him. He can learn it in small steps during
the first few years. By four he should be able to sit still
and be quiet. He may need to draw or color in a book.
By the time he is five he should be ready to sit still
without dropping things. Even then do not punish him
for some noise unless he does it on purpose.

I have some lovely things in my home. I love fine china and crystal. I spank my young child for touching things that are easy to break. How can I make her leave these things alone?

Do not punish children for doing things that come
naturally for them. They must do some of these things
in order to learn. They need to explore. They need
to touch things. It is how their minds grow. We enjoy
these nice things by looking at them. Children want
to touch them. They may even try to taste them and

smell them. They want to wave them around in the air. They may even want to throw them. By these things children learn about gravity. They learn what is rough and what is smooth. They also learn what makes mother angry.

You should not let your child tear up your home. But it is not right to think a child must not touch anything. Parents should not put some things where the child can reach them. Put away things that will break. Put away things that could harm the child. Let the child explore as much as you can. Don't spank him for things he does not know about. But some things he must learn. Stoves are hot. Television knobs should not be touched. Teach him what "Don't touch" means. A few slaps on the fingers will help him learn.

My daughter is three years old. She acts up at the grocery store. She runs when I call her. She begs for candy and gum. When I say no, she throws a tantrum. I don't want to punish her in the store. She knows that. What should I do?

Kids seem to know when they are in a place where you won't punish them. When they know that, they will not act as they do at home. I would talk with her on the next trip to the store. Tell her just what you expect. Make it clear that you mean business. Then when she acts up, take her to the car or behind the building. Then do what you would do if you were home. She will get the message.

My friend is a doctor. One of his patients was Robert. He was ten years old. The office staff did not look forward to Robert's visits. Each time he came, he nearly wrecked the office. The doctor saw one day that Robert had a very bad tooth. He knew he would have to send him to a dentist. But which one? He didn't want to send him to just any dentist. He didn't want the dentist angry with him. He knew what Robert would do to the dentist's office. At last he thought of someone. He was an older man. He knew all about kids.

Robert arrived at the dentist's office. The dentist said, "Get up in the chair."

"No chance," the boy said.

The dentist said, "Son, I told you to get in that chair. That is what I intend for you to do."

"If you make me get in that chair, I will take my clothes off," the boy said.

"Then take them off," the dentist said.

The boy took off his shirt and undershirt. Then he took off his shoes.

"Now get in the chair," the dentist said.

"I said I'd take off my clothes if you make me get in the chair."

"Take them off," the dentist said.

Then the boy took off the rest of his clothes.

"All right, now get in the chair," the dentist said.

The boy got into the chair, and the dentist took care of the bad tooth.

When it was over, the boy said, "Give me back my clothes."

"I'm sorry," said the dentist. "Tell your mother we are keeping your clothes here tonight. She can pick them up in the morning."

The boy was shocked. The waiting room door opened. The boy walked out to his mother with no clothes on. The room was filled with people. They were laughing at the boy. Robert and his mother walked past them and into the hall. They went down the elevator and into the parking lot. All the people laughed at him.

The next morning the mother came to the office. She wanted to talk to the dentist. She said, "I thank you for what you did. For years Robert has been doing this to people. He kept saying he would take off his clothes if he did not get his way. I didn't make him behave in public. I was afraid he would take them off. You were the first person who called his bluff. I don't think he will ever try that again."

I know you don't think toddlers should be spanked often. Is there another way to discipline kids that age?

One way is to make them sit in a chair. Make them sit down and tell them to think about what they did. Most kids that age want to run and play all the time. They hate to sit still for ten dull minutes. To some kids this will punish them more than a spanking. And they may think about it longer.

We have an adopted child. He came to us when he was two years old. He had been abused very badly. For the first two years we could not bring ourselves to spank him. Even when he deserved it we would not punish him. We are not his real parents anyway. We wonder if we have the right to punish him.

Parents who adopt often feel sorry for their new children. So they don't ever get control of them. They feel life has been too hard on the little ones. They don't want to make it worse for them. Such parents often feel they don't have the right to punish an adopted child. But these feelings are wrong. They can cause much trouble later on. Adopted kids have the same needs as those born to you. They need to be guided and trained just like others. You must treat them the same as any other child. Otherwise they will not feel secure. They will think they are not the same as other kids. You should not think they are poor kids who need special help. If you do, they will see themselves that way.

Some kids are sick and deformed. Their parents also find it hard to punish them. A child with a withered arm can still be a wild kid. Such a child may have parents who do not make him behave as well as other kids. All kids need to be controlled. They need to be taught how to act. Other problems do not take away from that need. You prove that you love the child by showing loving control.

CHAPTER 4

The Role of Discipline

Some say a child should be punished for doing wrong. If not, he may give his parents trouble all through life. Could that be true?

Often that is true. If a parent loses control in early conflicts, it becomes harder to win later. The parent who never wins is making a big mistake. Each time the parent gets weaker. The parent may be too tired or too weak to try. The child will soon reach his teens. The mistake will then come back to haunt the parent. You must make a child five years old pick up his toys. If not, you won't control him when he reaches his teens. The teen years are the most stubborn days of life. A child is made up of all the things he was taught. He must learn to behave in the first twelve years. If not, he will act much worse later on. A child who acted up twelve years ago could be like a time bomb. The best time to take the fuse out was twelve years before.

I am a teacher. My first year on the job was bad. I loved the students. I treated them as if they were my own kids. But they turned away when I

tried to show love. I could not control them. They had to test my strength and courage. Then they could accept my love. Why do you think this is true?

I don't know. But all good teachers will say the same thing. A child must first respect a person. Then he can accept love from him or her. You can't be easy at first and firm later. I once taught a class of college students. They were going to be teachers. I tried to tell them about this rule. They thought that if they just showed love, students would respect them. I knew what was going to happen. The students were going to throw love back in their face. They won't accept love until the giver has won their respect.

I believe God is the same way. First he told us how holy he was. He showed his wrath and justice. Then he showed us how much he loves us.

Some parents feel guilty. They don't make their kids show them respect. They think it will look like they are showing how strong and important they are. What do you think?

I don't agree. A child should respect his parents. This respect is the basis for the way he relates to others. He must learn to respect those over him. If not, he won't respect teachers. He will not respect the police or the law. He won't work well on the job or in the world.

You will want your child to accept your values. You must win his respect when he is young. A child who won't obey his parents will despise them later. "Stupid old Mom and Dad!" he will say. "I have them wound around my finger. Sure, they love me. But I think they are afraid of me." He may not say these things. But he feels them each time he wins over his parents. Later he will be more open about it. He won't respect his parents. And he won't want any part of what they believe.

Parents want their children to believe as they do. They want them to know about God. Parents must first get their kids to believe in them. If parents don't win kids' respect, kids won't respect their parents' God either. They won't accept their morals, their leaders, their country. Many problems today began like that. Kids lost respect for their parents. Then they do not respect their values. That becomes the generation gap.

We say that kids should respect their parents. Don't parents need to respect their children, too?

Yes, they do. A mother can't ask her child to treat her nicely if she doesn't do the same for him. She should be gentle with his ego. She should not put him down in front of his friends. She should punish him where others can't see him. Parents should not laugh at their children. The child may have strong feelings about some things. The parents should think about them. Parents should show that they really do care. Self-esteem is a very tender thing. It is very easy to damage. Little things can hurt a lot. A father may be sarcastic. He may be very critical. If he is, he won't get much respect in return. His kids may be afraid of him. But they will want to get even later on.

Some kids openly defy their parents. What are they thinking when they do?

Kids know what they are doing. That is why parents need to handle it well. When a child shows no respect, there is a reason. When he harms himself or others, he may be testing the limits. He is doing what the police do. They go by the shops at night. They try to open the doors. They want to know that they are all well locked. The child may be trying out his parents. He wants to know if the limits are certain. He can't feel secure if there are no limits. When the parents stand firm, a child knows the limits are firm.

What do a child's security and discipline have to do with each other? I have been reading what others have said. They think kids should grow up feeling free. They say kids should have more voice in how the home is run.

I have worked with children for more than twenty years. I am convinced that kids feel more sure of themselves if they have limits set for them. They need to know parents will enforce the rules of the home.

My family and I once drove across a long narrow bridge. The bridge is hundreds of feet high. The first time a person goes over it, he feels tense. Just think what it would be like if there were no rails on the bridge. Where would you steer the car? Right down the middle! You don't plan to hit the rails. But you feel more secure knowing they are there.

A child is like that too. A teacher at a nursery school made a test one day. He took down the fence around the yard where the kids played. He thought they would feel more free without a fence. It didn't work. The children clumped together in the middle of the yard. They didn't wander away. They didn't even go near the edge of the grounds. They felt more secure with the fence.

When there are limits, people feel secure. When the home is what it should be, the children live in safety. If they stay in the limits, they don't get into trouble. We are free if we keep the rules. That is what true democracy is. But it does not mean no limits.

People say that kids love justice. They are supposed to like law and order. Then why do I have trouble with my son? I try to reason with him about the things he does wrong. But he won't listen to me. I have to punish him to make him listen.

Kids respect strength and courage. This is true if strength comes with love. How else can you explain our kids' heroes? They like Superman and Wonder Woman. Why else would they say, "My dad can beat up your dad"? Boys and girls want to know who is the toughest. A new kid on the block has to prove himself. Those who work with kids know that there is a "top dog" in every group. And there will be one little pup at the bottom. All those in between know where they stand.

So kids respect strength and courage. That is why they want to know how "tough" their leaders are. They will often not obey you on purpose. They want to know what you will do. They want to know who is in charge. It does not matter who you are. You may be a parent or a grandparent. You may lead a Boy Scout troop or drive a bus. You may be a Brownie leader or a teacher. Sooner or later it will happen. One of your kids will clench his fists. He will challenge you as his leader.

This is a game I call "Challenge the Chief." Even young kids will play it. A father took his daughter to a basketball game. She was three years old. The little girl did not care about the game. She was watching other things. The father let her climb on the bleachers. He told her how far she could go. He showed her a line on the gym floor. "Don't go past that line," he said. He had just gone back to his seat. Her little game began. She walked toward the line. She stopped for a second. Then she grinned at her father. Then she placed one foot over the line. She was asking her father a question. "What are you going to do about it?" That question is asked of every parent who has ever lived.

We are all like that. We don't like to obey. God told Adam and Eve what they could do. One thing he told them not to do. "Do not eat this fruit," he said. That was the fruit they wanted to eat.

A parent who won't accept the child's challenge will have problems. Something changes between parent and child. The child no longer respects his parent. He thinks the parent is not worthy of his respect. He wonders why the parent won't make him obey. *If he loved me, he would,* he thinks.

It is a strange thing about kids. They want to be led by their parents. But they want their parents to earn the right to lead them.

We say we want kids who can control themselves. We want them to rely on themselves. Yet we control them from the outside. How do we get them to take over for themselves?

Many who write and talk about raising children think one should not punish children. They say kids should learn control by themselves. But I don't think kids are mature enough yet to do that. Left alone, kids would have neither outside discipline nor self-control. They would go through life without doing anything they don't like. Could you expect such a child to be self-disciplined later on? He would not even know the meaning of the word.

Parents should teach a child self-control. They do that by using outside control when he is young. The child should be made to behave well. By doing so he learns how to control himself. Then as he grows up, he learns to control himself more and more without being told. He is no longer forced to do what he learned. He does it because he knows it is right. For example, a child should be taught to keep his room neat. Then when he is older he should know how to do it himself. If not, the parent should close the door. They should let him live in a dump.

My parents punished me a lot when I was a child. I was afraid of them. My cousin was raised in a home with very few rules. She was a spoiled brat. Today she is still selfish. My parents were harsh. My cousin's parents were permissive. Explain how these types of homes affect kids growing up.

They both can harm a child. One is too harsh. Too much control shames a child. The home is cold and rigid. He lives all the time in fear of being punished. He is not able to decide things for himself. His ego is smashed under the boots of his parents' power. The child will depend on his parents all his life. He will also grow up angry with them. Later he may even have mental problems. But too little control can harm a child just as much. A child should not be his own master. The child will frustrate the mother. His behavior will be so bad she won't take him out in public. The child will have a hard time with authority later on. He won't listen to teachers or the police. He won't listen to his pastor. He won't even listen to God.

Both kinds of homes can be bad for a child. Too much control and punishment is wrong. Too much freedom can hurt the child. The best kind of parenting is somewhere in the middle.

You said that you think discipline should be based on the Bible. On what verses do you base your views? How do you deal with the will and the spirit of a child?

The Bible teaches about both. First, the parents help shape the child's will. The father must have control in his home. He should command the respect of his children (1 Timothy 3:4-5).

The parents should also protect the child's spirit. The Bible says, "Children, obey your parents." This was the first command of God to have a promise. God said, "Honor your father and mother . . . that you will have a long life." Fathers should not punish their children wrongly. If they do, it makes it hard for them to obey God's command (Ephesians 6:1-4).

CHAPTER 5

How to Discipline

I know I need to take charge of my kids. But I need to know how. Give me some step-by-step rules to follow.

There are six steps. They are very broad rules. But I think you should be able to use them.

First, set the limits before you start to enforce them. You must first tell the child what you expect. He needs to know them before you start to punish him. If you don't, he won't think you are just. If he gets a slap, he won't know what he did wrong. If you have not made the rule yet, don't punish him for breaking it.

Second, be calm and firm. The child may break the rule on purpose. He must know what you expect out of him. He should be made to answer for what he does wrong. That sounds easy, I know. Many kids will challenge their parents. They want to prove who is boss. A child will know what his parents want and expect. But he may choose not to obey them anyway. He knows he is taking a risk. These meetings of the will are sure to come. When they do, the parent must make sure that he wins. The child has made it clear what he is doing. He is looking for a fight. The parent must make certain that he gets it. The parent must not go to pieces. The parent must be calm but firm. The parent must not scream or burst into tears. If the parent loses the battle, he loses the child's respect.

Third, try to learn why the child did not obey. He may be willful. Or the child may forget or just be careless. They are not the same. So he should not be punished unless he does it on purpose. He may just forget to feed the dog. He may not think to take out the trash. Or he may leave his bike out in the rain. He is not doing these things on purpose. The parent must be gentle. But he must teach the child to do better. But if a child does not learn, the parent must help him. The child may have to work to pay for any damage he did. He may have the item taken away. But it won't be the same kind of punishment.

Fourth, encourage the child when the battle is over. Use that time to teach him. If the child has cried, he needs to be comforted. He needs lots of love at that time. Hold him close and tell him you love him. Tell him again why you had to punish him. These times build love and oneness. Christians should pray with their children at these times.

Fifth, don't ask the child to do things he can't do. Be sure your child can do what you demand of him. Don't spank him if he wets the bed. He may not be able to help it. Don't spank him if he is not potty-trained by one year of age. Make sure he can do the schoolwork before you scold him.

Sixth, let love guide you. All that you do must be done in love. Love will even cover up some of your mistakes.

My child has a strong will. I know I should teach him discipline. But I'm afraid I will break his spirit. I don't want to damage his emotions. Can I discipline him when he does not behave well without hurting his self-concept?

Shaping a child's will is one thing. Breaking his spirit is another. Don't confuse the two. The human spirit refers to self-esteem. It refers also to a person's sense of worth. The human spirit is very fragile. No matter how old we are, it can be damaged. You are right. It is easy to break a child's spirit. Ridicule can do it. If you show no respect, or hold back love, the child's spirit suffers. Anything that lowers his self-esteem harms his spirit.

But the will is made of steel. It comes strong from birth. A baby wants to control things around him from the very start.

Later on, the child's will will get even stronger. Some kids will hold their breath until they faint. If you have seen a child do this, you know how well it works. One mother told me about her son. He was three years old. He got angry with her. He refused to eat for two days.

The mother was very worried about him. She began to feel guilty. At last the father stepped in. He looked the child in the eye. He told him to eat or he was going to get a good spanking. The contest was over. The child began to eat.

I have wondered why more has not been said about this kind of child. I think some people don't believe children can be evil. They think that the little ones are filled with goodness. They think they learn to be evil. They hold a very rosy view of children. To them I say, "Take another look!"

What is the mistake parents make most often in disciplining their kids?

I think that it is the wrong use of anger. Anger is not a good way to control boys and girls. It won't work with any age. Yet many parents use it to make their kids behave. I once heard a well-known teacher talk about her work. She said she likes being a teacher. But she hates the daily task of teaching. "The children are so unruly," she said. "I have to stay mad at them all the time. If I don't, I can't control them." How hard it must be to be mean and angry just to do your job. Yet many teachers know no other way to teach. I can tell you, it doesn't work!

Think what would happen if you were a police- man. You have no patrol car. You do not have a badge or carry a gun. You don't have a uniform. And you can write no tickets. All you can do is stand on the corner. You can yell and scream at the drivers who broke the law. Do you think people would slow down? Would your anger do any good? You would only look funny and foolish.

But a driver knows the sight of a policeman. He knows what the flashing lights on his car mean. When he stops his car, the man in uniform gets out. He looks courteous. He walks with dignity. "Sir," he says, "you were going sixty miles an hour. This is a thirty-mile-per-hour zone. May I see your driver's license?" He opens his notebook. He takes out a ticket and begins to write. He does not look angry. He does not criticize you. Yet you go to pieces. You look through your wallet. Your hands are moist. Your mouth is dry. Why is your heart thumping? Because of the *action* the policeman is about to take.

Discipline changes behavior. Anger does not. In fact, most adult anger does more harm than good. It causes the children to lose respect for the parent. They see that the parent has no control over what is happening. We are the agents of justice for our children. Did you ever see a judge in tears or losing his temper? No. This is why the court system works. It is objective, rational, and dignified.

This does not mean that teachers should not have feelings. It doesn't mean parents should not show emotion. But anger is not the way to change a child's behavior.

My husband and I are divorced. I have to do all of the disciplining of our children. Do I handle it the same as if the kids had two parents?

Yes. The rules about good discipline are the same. But it will be harder for you. You do not have anyone to support you. When the children rebel, you must be both mother and father. That is not easy. The children won't make it easy for you because you are alone. You must demand their respect. If you don't, you won't get it.

Many people are against spanking kids today. They say parents should not hit a child. It will teach them to hit others. What do you think?

I was on a television show a few years ago. I had to debate with another doctor. He did not think it was right to spank. He said that spanking causes a lot of the violence in this country. We could stop this violence if we quit spanking our kids. He said spanking told kids that hitting others was all right.

I think it is silly to blame all that on spanking. Look at all the killing on television. Hundreds of killings are shown every year. Why don't people blame these shows?

Four reasons are given not to spank. First, some think it makes kids want to hit others. They say spanking is a hostile act. They claim parents punish because they are angry. They do it to hurt the children. I don't agree with these reasons. It is true that some spanking is wrong. Angry parents often spank wrongly. This kind really does hurt the child. But that is not what a good parent does. Parents should spank because they love their kids. They do it to keep their kids from worse harm.

A child can learn from being punished. Think of a child near a hot stove. If he touches it, he will get burned. But he has learned from it. He won't touch it again. That is what a spanking can do. The same thing happens when a child falls down. A dog bite will teach him not to go near grumpy dogs. He gets hurt from these things. But they do not destroy his self-esteem. They do not make him violent. They just teach him what he can and can't do. Being spanked works the same way. It tells a child things to avoid. He learns not to be selfish.

Second, some say parents spank when they don't know what else to do. They say spanking is the last thing we should try. I don't agree. Parents should spank when a child disobeys on purpose. It is better to spank when the child first disobeys. It is better to spank before the child makes you angry. If you wait, the child will sass and pout for hours. Then you will get angry. And that is the wrong time to spank. I think people who don't believe in spanking cause child abuse. They take away a parent's right to punish. Then the child keeps up his bad behavior. By then the parent hits the child in anger. That kind of spanking is child abuse.

Third, others say that punishment doesn't work. Tests have been made with rats. When rewarded, the rats did what the testers wanted. But they didn't respond to electric shocks. But kids and rats are not the same. Rats don't rebel as a child can. I agree in part. I don't think that an electric shock would help a child learn. I would not shock a child to teach him to pronounce a word right. I don't think he would learn from that. But if a child chooses not to obey, he can learn from a spanking.

Fourth, others say spanking lowers a child's self-worth. Spanking takes away his dignity. But I don't agree. A child knows if his parents love him. It will show in the way they spank him. That is why some kids seem relieved when they are spanked. If they know they deserve it, they get over it very quickly. They know why they got punished. It helps them control their urges to do wrong.

A father once took his family to a restaurant. His son was five years old. The boy began to talk back to his mother. He flipped water on his younger brother. He was making trouble on purpose. His father warned him four times. But he did not stop. His father took him by the hand. He led him out to the parking lot. He began to spank him. A woman followed them out. She was a meddler. She screamed at the father. She shook her finger at him. "Stop," she yelled. "Turn him loose. If you don't stop, I will call the police." The boy looked at his father. He said, "What's wrong

with that woman?" He knew why he was getting
spanked. He knew better than the woman.

But don't use just spanking for punishment. Spanking is not the right thing to do all the time. Other
things should be tried also. A wise parent knows just
what a child needs.

I have a very willful toddler. How should I spank him?

Mild spanking can begin early. About fifteen to
eighteen months is not too early. You should not
do it often. And you should use it only when the child
is not obeying. Don't punish him for being a child.
Kids need to try out the world around them. They
should be taught to obey. They must learn to yield to
their parents. But they won't learn that in one day.

Spank with a little switch or a belt. Do not use your
hand. The hand should be used to show love. Some
parents slap their children. The kids are not expecting
it. Then one day the parent will reach up to scratch his
ear. The child will jump. He will think he is about to
be slapped.

Should a spanking hurt? Yes, or else it will do no
good. That does not mean that you should damage
him. Two or three stings on the legs or bottom is
enough. Tell him when you do it, "You must obey me."
And spank right after it happens. If you wait too long,
he won't know why it happened. After the spanking
the child may cry. When he is done, he may want to

come to you. Let him come. Put your arms around him and rock him softly. Tell him how much you love him. And tell him again why you had to spank him. This is as important as the spanking. This is also a good time to pray with the child.

CHAPTER 6

Self-Esteem in Children

I have always had poor self-esteem. How did I get this way? When did it begin?

It began when you were very young. A child needs to prove his worth. He wants to be sure about his place in the home. Later he wants to be accepted outside the home. The way others respond tells him what to think about himself. As a small child, he knows if others think he is ugly or strange. He can tell if he is needed or loved.

These feelings stay with him. They don't affect him much during the first twelve years. But he collects more bad feelings during that time. He still hears bad things about himself. Each time he fails, he adds it to the record. He remembers each unkind thing said to him. Then he enters his teens. That is when the trouble begins. All these bad thoughts come out. He then deals with those feelings for the rest of his life.

Parents should help build the child's self-esteem. What keeps them from doing it?

Our world teaches people to worship beauty and brains. Parents are what our world has made them. They expect a lot from their kids. At times they may expect too much of them. A parent may have poor self-esteem. He won't accept that his child has a problem. In fact, he may cover up how he feels about such a child. He will see the ugly child as a picture of himself. The child may be deformed or not strong mentally. The parent may not be able to accept a child. He can't say to the child, "I love you. You have great worth to me."

How do you as a parent help a child's self-esteem? First, you must change the way you think. You should not feel let down because of your child. Do you think he is dumb? Have you rejected him? Was he born at a bad time? Did his coming cause you money problems? Did you want a boy instead of a girl? Does the child make you feel ashamed?

A child will respect himself if his parents respect him. If you don't like him, he can't like himself. Find out about your own feelings.

My daughter is nine years old. She lacks confidence. How can I help her build self-respect?

One way is to teach her how to use her strengths. Children will be weak in some ways. And they are strong in others. They need to find their strengths. They must learn how to balance one with the other.

Our job as parents is to help children find their strengths. Then we must teach them how to use them. If a child does not find his strengths, he will feel weak. He will think he is not as good as others. Sometimes it is good for a child to see how weak he is. It will often make him work harder. It depends on the child. Boiling water can make an egg hard. Or it can make a carrot soft.

The question is, how will your daughter's weakness affect her? Will she break under the weight? Or will it make her work harder? It may depend on how you help her. She may feel bad about a weakness. Can you help her find a strength? It may be music or art. She may learn to write or cook. The key is to start her young. Help her to do well in something. If a teenager has no skills, her ego will suffer. Your daughter needs something that she does well. She needs to say, "I may not be the most popular student. But I am the best trumpet player."

Some kids are hateful and mean. They often pick on children with a handicap. Some handicapped children may be hurt. They have no defense against mean humor. Should adults try to help these children?

Yes, they should. I know what you are talking about. In fact, I once did something hurtful. I was in a Sunday school class. I was about eight years old. One day a new boy came to class. His name was Fred.

He had strange-looking ears. They were curved like the letter *C*. His ears reminded me of the fenders on a Jeep. It was during the war. We all knew what Jeeps looked like. I did something very thoughtless. I pointed to his ears and laughed. I turned to my friends. I called Fred "Jeep Fenders." We all thought it was funny. But Fred didn't laugh. He got very red in the face. He jumped to his feet and ran for the door. He was crying as he reached the hall. He ran from the building. He never came back to the class.

I remember how shocked I was. I had no idea I shamed him so badly. I was a thoughtful kid. But I had never thought about how it would hurt a person to laugh at him. My mother has since said she should have taught me to feel for others. I don't remember what we were reading in Sunday school then. But we should have been reading, "Love thy neighbor as thyself."

My daughter is six years old. I want to get her ready for the esteem problems she will face as a teen. She will be under a lot of social pressure. How can I help her?

All of childhood is for getting ready for the teen years. Parents have ten years to help their kids. Kids must learn values and attitudes during these years. These will help them cope with problems as adults. We should help young kids to know what self-worth means and how to gain it. All of us have to deal with self-worth some time in life.

The teaching should start before school age. When your child meets a very shy child, you should talk about it. "Why do you think Billie is too shy to tell you what he is feeling? Do you think he doesn't have much self-confidence?" Use the word *confidence* a lot. Tell your child it means "courage" and "belief in oneself." Your child will be taking part in school and church plays. Say nice things about how well she did.

As the child grows older, try to point out bad examples of self-confidence. Say, "Did you notice Denise this morning? Did you see how silly she acted? She was trying to make people look at her, wasn't she? Why do you think she did that? Why does she have to be noticed by everyone? Do you think Denise likes herself? She wants people to like her. But she doesn't think they do. Why don't you try to make friends with her? Maybe you can make her feel better about herself. Would you like to invite her to spend the night?"

With this kind of help, your child will learn about how others feel. You will also help her understand her own feelings. Each year she should know better how to deal with her feelings of weakness.

You have only a few years to teach your child. In that time she should learn four things. First, all kids don't like themselves at times. Second, most feel ugly and dumb at times. They feel their friends don't accept them. Third, times of self-doubt won't last long. Fourth, all of us have great value because we are God's children.

I think these are healthy ways to help your child. They will help her to understand other humans. I once heard why many people lose their jobs. It was not because they could not do their jobs well. Eighty percent were fired because they could not get along with people. We can help our kids now to understand other people. It will help them keep their dignity and sense of worth.

Other kids on our block make fun of my son. He comes home crying. He gets very depressed. How can I help him when this happens?

Your son needs a good friend. You can be that to him. Let him talk. Don't try to tell him that it does not hurt. And don't say it is silly to be hurt by what they say. Ask him if he knows why they don't like him. He may be causing the problem. He may be trying to lord something over them. They may think your son is selfish or not honest. Try to understand what he is going through. But don't cry yourself or give up hope. Try to play a game with him. Do something he will enjoy. And try to do something to get at the cause of the problem.

Have your son invite one of these boys to go to the zoo one day. Or offer some other fun time. Let this boy spend the night at your house. It may be that even the worst child on the block will start being kind. It will help your child to make friends. And it may help you to see if your son is making some mistakes. He may be driving these friends away by the things he does. When you know these things, it will help you to help him. He may need to improve how he gets along with others.

You have said that our value system in this country is bad. It hurts the self-esteem and mental health of our children. What changes can we make to improve our kids' emotional health?

Most people's emotional problems come from two things. First, they come from bad homes. Their families were not loving. Their parents did not meet their emotional needs. Second, these people don't know how to get along with others. They have no respect from their peers. People do not accept them. Most emotional problems can be traced to these bad relations. The worst hurts come during the first twenty years of their lives.

The best way to help kids is to teach them to love and respect others. You yourself must show them this love and respect. Kids do not know how to feel for others. Parents let their kids be unkind. They let them get away with being mean to other kids. They don't stop them from teasing even ugly or handicapped kids. They mistreat the foreign child or the minority kid. The harm they do could last a lifetime.

Adults should teach love and dignity. We should insist that our kids be kind to others. Young children are easy to hurt. They have more feelings than adults.

But kids learn how to be vicious. Kids are mean to
each other because adults have not taught them better.

A woman once told me about what happened in her
school. Her daughter was in fourth grade. She was the
room mother. It was Valentine's Day. That day can be
very painful for some children. Each child counts the
number of valentines he gets. It is how he measures his
social worth. The teacher said the class was to play a
game. The game was to be played with boy-girl teams.
Fourth graders don't often play well with mixed sexes.
The teacher asked the kids to pair up. All the boys
looked at one girl. She was very homely. The boys all
laughed and pointed to her. She was overweight. Her
teeth stuck out in front. She was too shy to look at
anyone.

"Don't put us with Hazel," the boys said.
"Anybody but Hazel! She'll give us a disease!"

The mother waited for the teacher to help the girl.
But the teacher said nothing. The teacher ignored
Hazel.

I think that teacher was wrong. I would have done
something to those boys. I would have said, "Wait a
minute. Who gave you the right to say such mean
things to Hazel? Which one of you is perfect? I know
you very well. I know about your homes. I have your
school records. I know some of your secrets. Would
you like me to share them with the class? That way we
can laugh at you. I could do it. I could make you want
to crawl into a hole and hide. But listen to me. You

don't have to be afraid. I will never embarrass you that way. Why not? Because it hurts to be laughed at. It hurts more than a stubbed toe or a cut finger. I have a question for you who were laughing. Have you ever had a group of children make fun of you? If you haven't, then brace yourself. Someday it will happen to you. Sooner or later you will say something dumb. And they will point at you. Then they will laugh in your face. And when it happens, I want you to think of what you did today."

Then I would say this to the whole class. "Let's learn from what happened today. First, we will not be mean to each other in this class. We will laugh together when things are funny. But we will not do it by making one person feel bad. Second, I will never make any of you feel bad in this class. You can count on that. Each of you is a child of God. He molded you with his loving hands. He has said that we all have equal worth. That means that Suzie is no better or worse than Mary or Charles. You may think you are better than others. That isn't true. Each of you is priceless to God. And each of you will live forever. That is how much you are worth. God wants us to be kind to others. We are going to do that for the rest of this year."

If a teacher would do that, the kids would learn some very good things. They would learn that they are all safe. "If Hazel, who is overweight, is safe, then I am safe too," they could say. They would know three things. First, "The teacher has no pets." Second, "The teacher respects all of us." Third, "Teacher will fight for any of us who is being treated badly."

Parents, take up for the weak child on your block. Let the others know they can't pick on him. Show them that you will speak up for him. Tell them why you are doing it. Make all the kids feel safe. Don't be afraid to take the lead on behalf of a weak child. You can't find a better way to spend your time.

I find it hard to let go of my kids. Should I feel this way?

Letting go of kids is one of the hardest tasks for parents. A good motto is "Hold them close. Then let them go." Parents should stay involved with their kids. Children need the parents' love and care. They need control and discipline. But then they reach their teens and twenties. Then you must let them go. It is a scary time for Christian parents. They care about the spiritual lives of their kids. They ask, "Did I train them well? Are they ready to be on their own?" Some Christian parents try to hang on. They try to protect their sons and daughters from things that would harm them. But it is better to let them go. They will make fewer mistakes on their own. If parents try to control, the children rebel. That causes even more trouble. There is a proverb I like. It is not from the Bible. But it is a good one. "If you love something, set it free. If it comes back to you, then it is yours. If it doesn't return, it wasn't yours in the first place."

I once found a young coyote. He had strayed down from the mountains near our home. I caught him in my backyard. I was able to put a collar on him. All the kids around us came to look at him. I thought I would try to make a pet out of him. But I talked to someone who knew all about coyotes. He said I would never be able to do it. Coyotes raised in the wild stay wild. He said he would never get tame.

I turned the coyote over to the game warden. He took him back to the place he came from. I had to turn him loose. He would be no fun tied up against his will.

Love has to be free. It is true with man and his pets. It is true between people. The fastest way to destroy love is to put the loved one in a cage. You can't demand love. It must be given freely. Think back to your dating days. One person would begin to worry about losing the other. One would start calling six or eight times a day. One might hide behind trees to watch the other one. A breakup would come when that began. Love must have freedom.

Even God gives us a choice. He does not make us love him. He wants us to come to him because we want to be with him. He said, "I love all who love me. Those who look for me shall surely find me" (Prov. 8:17). That is the love that comes from freedom.

The same is true with our older children. There comes a time when our work as parents is over. As I did with the coyote, you must take off the collar. You must let your child go free. If he runs away, he runs away. If he marries the wrong person, he marries the wrong person. He must make his own choices.

Those teen years are not easy. They are hard for the parent. They are also hard for the child. The key is to lay a good foundation. Then when the time comes, face it with courage. It is healthy if the child rebels a little. That is what makes him learn to stand on his own. It would not be healthy if he never wanted to leave home. When the child becomes an adult, he cannot remain a child. Some strain between parents and children is part of God's plan.

CHAPTER 7

Growing Up

My son is in junior high. He does not know how to be responsible. He will be grown someday. How can I teach him now?

Kids must know that they pay for what they do. They have to answer for their actions. This is one goal of parenting. You must teach these truths when they are young. That is part of what is wrong with the world today. People don't think they should answer for what they do. A child is three years old. He will scream at his mother. The mother does nothing. A child is in first grade. He will attack his teacher. The teacher says, "He is just a child." She does nothing. A boy is ten years old. He steals candy from a store. They catch him and turn him over to his parents. They do nothing. A child is fifteen years old. He takes the keys to the family car. He gets arrested. The father comes and pays the fine. A boy is seventeen. He drives his car like a crazy person. He wrecks the car. His parents pay to have it fixed. All through life the child acts poorly. His parents don't make him pay for any of it. They say that they don't because they love him.

People like that grow up thinking there is no price to pay. They don't learn that every move they make affects the future. Bad behavior should bring sorrow and pain. But they never learned these truths. Such a person goes to get a job. He gets to work late three times during the first week. After some angry words, his boss fires him. This time Mom and Dad can't help him. But many parents try, even at that age. The result is a person who stays a child all his life.

How do you teach responsibility to a child? First you let the child suffer when he does wrong. When he acts badly, he should be punished. He may waste time in the morning. If he misses the bus, let him walk a mile or two to school. If your girl loses her lunch money, let her miss a meal. But don't be too harsh. Don't expect too much of small children. But let them feel the pain that comes with doing wrong.

My children are four and five years old. A few days ago, my husband and I went out to dinner. We were leaving the house. My two children started to cry. I gave them each a piece of candy. They stopped crying. We were able to leave in peace. Was that the right way to do it?

I would say no. That was not a reward for being good. That was paying them for being childish. You taught your kids to cry for what they want. Next time you leave, you will have to give them more candy.

You do not want to reward a child for the wrong things. Think of what would happen in this case. A man and his wife are having guests for dinner. They have a child who is three years old. They put the child to bed at seven o'clock. They know the child will cry. But what can they do? The guest comes. The child starts to cry. At first he cries softly. Then he gets louder and louder. At last the mother lets the child get out of bed. Now what has she taught the child? He has learned that the louder he cries, the quicker he will get what he wants. From now on, that mother will have a battle with her child. She should expect to hear a lot of crying from him.

Think about this mother. She has a teenager named Betty. Betty never takes no for an answer. She acts poorly all the time. Betty will ask to go somewhere. Sometimes it may be a party. The mother is not sure what to say. At first she says Betty can't go. She does this to have time to think it over. She can always change her mind. But it is hard to go the other way. She can't say she can go and then change and say she can't go. Betty begs and complains. The more she does, the more likely her mother will change her mind. Many parents make this kind of mistake. They allow the child to argue and pout. Then after a lot of arguing, they give in. Parents should make up their minds before they speak. They should say yes or no. Then they should stick by what they say. If they don't, they teach their children to argue and beg.

Look at some other parents. They have a child seven years old. He wants to make his parents notice him. He does not know a good way to do it. At the table his mother says, "Eat your beans." He says, "No, I won't eat those rotten beans." He now has the eyes and ears of his parents. That is what he wanted. The mother could even make things worse. She could say, "If you eat your beans, I'll give you a treat."

A parent must be careful. He must be patient. But he should not let a child get away with bad behavior.

I know that I need to teach my son about sex before he grows up. But what else should I tell him?

He needs to know about the changes taking place in his body. Many young people don't know what is happening to them. All young people do not mature at the same rate. Some changes come and the young people don't know they are coming. They worry about them when they come. The other group knows the changes will come. But they come late for them. This group has fears and doubts when change doesn't come. Parents should talk to their kids about these changes. They should know before the fears come.

What are some of the changes that will come?

There are four things you must talk about with children.

1. They will start to grow at a faster rate. When it happens, they won't feel strong. They won't have much energy. They will need more sleep and food than when they were younger.
2. Their bodies will start to change. Their sex organs will become more mature. Hair will start to grow. Boys will worry about the size of their penis. The size is not really important. But boys think it is. A boy needs to know that the size does not affect his having sex when he grows up. Girls' breasts will start to grow larger. They need to know that the size of their breasts is also not really important.
3. They need to know about the menstrual cycle. Girls should know about it before it starts. It can frighten a girl if she does not know it is coming. Books and films can be used to help them. But parents should help them feel at ease about it.
4. They need to know about puberty. Tell them it does not come at the same age for all people. For boys it can come as early as twelve. Or it can come as late as nineteen. For girls it can begin at ten. Or it may be as late as seventeen. It is just the way some bodies mature.

What are the hardest years of growing up?

The years of thirteen and fourteen. During this time young people have many doubts. They feel they are not as good as others. A lot of social pressure is on them. They feel no self-worth. They want others to accept them. But acceptance is very hard to win. They fear others will reject them. It hurts to be laughed at. The least sign of being made fun of hurts a lot. It makes them feel even more like failures. It hurts to have no one to sit with on the school bus. It hurts not to be invited to parties. They worry about their looks. Then they wake up with seven new pimples. A boy may have thought a girl liked him. But that day she slaps his face. Boys and girls face these failures day after day. They never forget the hurt caused by them.

These years affect a child's mental health more than any other years. Some kids go off to junior high healthy and happy. They come out feeling broken and hopeless.

Junior high kids can be hard on each other. They attack a weak child. They are like wolves who live in the far north. Wolves look for a weak animal to attack.

It is sad to watch a weak child being attacked. Each of them comes from God. They are fresh from God's hands. God made them and loves them. But the kids in school teach them to hate themselves. They end up not liking their bodies. Some even wish they had not been born.

My son has low self-esteem. It hurts me to watch him. He is in junior high now. I know he has a hard time. Can you help me? I want to

know if he will come through it all right. Is he going to ruin his life now?

I know I have said that these years are very hard for kids. But there is a good side to it. We grow a lot through hard times. Both you and your son should think about that. Just make sure that he is not crushed by the hard things.

Where is the best place for a child to grow up? It is not where he will have no hard times. The best place is where there are a few hard problems. So don't try to take away all your son's problems. Let him learn to solve some of them by himself. He needs to learn how to face them on his own.

I grew up more or less a happy child. I didn't have many cares. I knew I was loved. My schoolwork was all right. All my life has been happy and joyful. But there were two very bad years. They were when I was in the seventh and eighth grades. I was about thirteen or fourteen.

I had big social problems. I felt that I was no good. I had all kinds of self-doubt. But I know those two years meant a lot to me. They added a lot to my growth. They helped make me who I am as an adult. I learned to feel for others going through hard times. It was then I decided I wanted to succeed in life. I know now why people feel inferior. I think I know more about how to talk to kids. It was because I had problems at that age. Who would have thought any good could come of all my problems? Yet I know my hurts back then taught me a lot.

I know this is hard to accept at the time. Your child needs these feelings of letdown. Through them he will learn to solve problems. He will know how to face trials. A child is like a tree. Some grow up in forests where there is lots of rain. These trees do not have long roots. They are easy to knock down by the wind. But a tree that grows in a dry place has long roots. They go deep into the ground. The tree becomes very strong. The winds will not knock it down.

Children are that way. Those who learn to solve problems grow strong. Parents must help them to grow strong. So do not take away all the things that cause them problems. You must encourage your children when they are hurt. You must give them the tools to solve their problems. But they must solve them by themselves.

Our son is fifteen years old. He is angry all the time. He is angry with both of us. He is angry with his sisters. He is angry at the world. We don't think we do anything to make him this way. Other parents tell me their children are the same way. Why are kids this age so angry? They seem to hate those who love them the most.

Part of the problem is their age. They are at the in-between stage. They are not adults. And they are not children. They don't get to do the things adults do. Yet they don't get away with things as younger kids do. Look at the way most kids are when they are fifteen. They see all the ads of the things adults can do. Yet they are said to be "too young" to enjoy them. They can't drive or drink. They can't work or leave home. They have sexual desires. Yet they can't do anything about them. All they can do is stay in school. There they can only read boring schoolbooks.

That is not really the way it is. But that is how they look at it. They feel they don't belong. They are angry because they don't think these things are fair.

There are other reasons they seem angry. Their bodies are going through change. Their bodies are putting out hormones. These often affect the way a person feels. I have seen many kids this age. I see many of them go through the same things. It seems to come at about the same time. That is why I believe it is caused by the changes in their bodies.

I know my kid is going through this hard time. He shows us no respect. But I have to put some limits on him. Tell me how.

Yes, your child needs limits during this time. But you should not insult him. You should not add to his problems. I learned this lesson when I was teaching junior high school. I saw that I could put all sorts of rules on the students. But I had to treat them right. I had to show them dignity and respect. I made friends of them. But I had to earn it. In and out of class, I was tough when they challenged me. But I was kind in all I did. I did not insult them. I stood up for the underdogs. And I tried to build up each one of them. I wanted them all to feel confident. They had to have self-respect. But I did not let down my standards. They came into my classroom. But they did not talk during class. They did not chew gum. They showed respect to each other. They did not curse or stick each other with pens.

You have to be kind but firm. I enjoyed those years. I loved my students and I think they loved me. I missed them when the weekends came. My wife never knew why I felt this way. At the end of the year I felt sad. There were tears shed by the kids when the year was over. And I shed a few of my own.

My son is fourteen. He is starting to rebel. He was never like that before. He breaks all the rules. He seems to hate his whole family. He got home late the other night. He refused to tell us where he was. How should I deal with this?

I suggest you take your son out to breakfast one day. Leave the rest of the family at home. It would be best to do this at a time when there is not much trouble. Don't do it in the middle of a big hassle. Tell him that you have some important things to talk about. But don't tell him what they are before the time. Here are some things I would say to him.

1. Son, I want to talk to you today. There are some changes taking place in you and in our home. We both know that the last few weeks have not been

happy. You have not enjoyed them, and we haven't either. You have been angry most of the time. You have not obeyed the rules. And you have been rude. Your mother and I have not done well either. We have been angry. And we have said things we were sorry about later. This is not what God wants our family to be like. This is not the way parents should be. And this is not the way a son should be. We must find a better way to solve our problems. That is why we are here this morning.

2. I want you to know what is going on. You have come to a new period in your life. It is called adolescence. This is the last part of being a child. And it is often very hard for kids and their parents. Nearly all people in the world go through it. And you are right on schedule. You could have seen many of these problems coming. That is what growing up will do. You have many pressures on you today. We want you to know that we understand. These last few months have been very hard. But we love you as much as we ever did.

3. This is what is taking place. You are old enough to have a taste of freedom. You are tired of being a little boy. You don't like being told what to wear and when to go to bed. You don't want others telling you what to eat. This is the way it should be at this age. Now you want to be your own boss. You want to make your own choices. You don't want others to tell you what to do. You are fourteen

now. You will be grown in just a few years. We won't have to be responsible for you then. The day is coming when you will marry. You will choose the girl you want. You will go to any school you choose. You will find the job you want. Your mother and I won't make any of these choices for you. We will let you be an adult. The closer you get to that age, the more freedom we plan to give you. You have many privileges now. You have more than you did last year. Next year you will have even more. We will soon set you free. You will then answer only to God.

4. But you must understand this. You are not grown yet. During the last few weeks you have wanted us to leave you alone. You want to stay out half the night. You want to fail in school if you like. You want to have no responsibility. And you have been angry when you didn't get your way. You have wanted us to treat you as if you were twenty-one. But you are only fourteen. You want to have your shirts ironed and meals on the table. You want us to pay your bills. You want the best of both worlds. But you don't want to be responsible. So what are we to do? It would be easy to let you have your own way. That is what many parents have done. But we won't do that. You are not ready to be on your own yet. We would hate you and not love you if we gave in to you now. We would be sorry for our mistake the rest of our lives.

You have younger sisters who are watching you.
We must protect them from the things you are
showing them. *This makes it sound as if they are responsible for the younger sibs when the younger sibs go through this. However it may be easier for parents if the younger sibs see that the parents mean business, just as in the example of older sibs*

5. Son, God has made us your parents. We must answer to him. We must do what is right for you. There is a story in the Bible about a man called Eli. It is found in the book of First Samuel. His sons would not obey God. The Bible is very clear. God was angry with Eli because he did not make his sons obey. God let Eli's sons get killed. But he also punished Eli. It is clear all through the Bible. God expects parents to discipline their children.

6. This is what I plan to do now. I want to make a pledge to you. I promise that from now on your mother and I will try even harder to be sensitive to your needs. We will try to think of your feelings. We are not perfect. You know that. But I know you may think we are not being fair with you. If so, *but in a respectful way.* you should tell us. We will talk about it. If you ask to do some new thing I will ask myself some questions. I will ask, "Can I give this to him? Is he ready for it? Will it harm him to have it?" If I can, I will give it to you. I will bend as far as I can.

7. But you must know the other side. There will be times when I must say no. And when I say no, I will be like a rock. You may get angry. You may slam doors and lose your temper. But I will not change. You may want to fight me about these rules. But I promise you will lose. You are too big

69

to spank. But I can make you sorry. I have the courage to do it. And my mind is made up. I will do my job these last years you are home. Now it is up to you. We will have a peaceful time at home. Or we can spend your last years at home fighting. Either way, you will get home when you are told. And you will carry your part of the load at home. And you will respect your mother and me.

8. Let me say it again. We love you as much as we ever did. We are going to stay friends through this. There is a lot of pain in the world today. Life is filled with hurts. There is loss and sickness and rejection. And in the end there is death. You have not hurt much in your life. But you will taste it soon enough. We need each other. We need you, and you still need us. That is what we want to tell you today.

9. Now, do you need to say things to us?

You will need to shape these thoughts to fit your needs. You won't use these very words. The needs of your sons or daughters will not be the same. They will not respond the same. Some kids may be open and ready to talk. Others may sit and hang their heads. But it does not matter. You have put the cards on the table. What you plan to do has been explained.

My daughter is fourteen. She wants to date a boy who is seventeen. I am not sure what to say. What should I tell her?

I would try to work out a plan with her. And tell her why you are doing it. You may say, "You are now just fourteen. I know now that you are thinking more about boys. That is how it was supposed to be. But you are not yet ready for a boy that old. A boy that old will ask you to do some things." If she asks you what you mean, tell her.

Tell her that you want to help her get ready for dating. There are some steps in between that she must take. First, tell her she must learn how to be friends with a boy. That comes before learning how to be a lover with one. She should start by meeting boys and girls her age, in groups. Say, "We will invite them to our house in groups. Or you can go to the homes of others to meet in groups. Then when you are fifteen or sixteen you can double-date. But it will be at places where there are older people. Then you can go on single dates when you are sixteen."

Tell her, "We want you to date and have fun with boys. We want to do the right thing. But you are not ready to date a boy this old. We will have to find other ways to meet your social needs."

CHAPTER 8

Kids Ask

I am fourteen years old. I have crummy looking pimples all over my face. What causes them? How can I get rid of them?

Your whole body is affected by the changes going on in your body. Even your skin changes during this time. Both boys and girls have the problem. It may be one of the worst things about this age. A study on teenagers was done not long ago. Two thousand kids were asked the same question: "What do you most dislike about yourself?" Skin problems was the answer given most.

These pimples are caused by oil in the skin. You will have more of it at this age than any other time. The oil comes out of the pores of your skin. The pores may get blocked up. When they do, the oil gets hard. It causes what is called blackheads. You will have this problem for several years. Some kids have it worse than others.

This skin problem is called acne. If you have it, you must take good care of your skin. Try to keep it clean. Keep oil and dirt off your face. Some think that eating greasy foods makes it worse. Doctors now think that is not true. If you have really bad problems, you might ask to see a skin doctor. These doctors are able to help the problem.

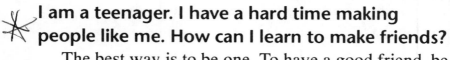

I am a teenager. I have a hard time making people like me. How can I learn to make friends?

The best way is to be one. To have a good friend, be a good friend. That is an old proverb. But it is still true. Most people feel a little inferior. They have self-doubts. That fact will help you to know the secret. Never make fun of others. Don't laugh at them. Let them know you respect them. They want you to accept them. Let them know they are important to you. Try to think about their feelings. Don't let people say mean things about them. And don't talk about them to others. You will see that they will do the same for you.

I am thirteen years old. I feel bad about myself. Is there anything I can do?

You are not alone. Look around you and see others who feel the way you do. Look at the kids in your school. Watch them as they come and go. You will see that many of them also feel inferior. They have doubts. Many of them are shy and quiet. Others show it by being angry and mean. Others act silly. Others are afraid to take part in games. Look at how many of them blush. Some act proud and stuck up. Look at how they act. If you look closely, you will see something. These are all signs of feeling inferior. You will see that it is a common problem. When you see that others feel as you do, you won't feel alone anymore. It is as if you are all sitting in a boat. The boat is leaking. You are all trying to plug the holes. I know. I nearly drowned in my own leaky boat when I was your age.

Look at the things that worry you. These things keep eating away in the back of your mind. What causes you to see a black cloud over you? Get off by yourself and think about it. List all the things that you don't like about yourself. You can be open and honest. No one else is going to see your list unless you show them. Write down the things that have been bothering you. Admit that there are things about yourself that you don't like. Maybe you get angry and blow up at people. Write it down.

Think about the worst of these problems. Do you get angry with people? Then do you feel bad about it later? Or are you shy? Does it make you afraid when you are with other people? Do you feel that you can't say the things you want to say? Do you think you are lazy? Are you unkind? Do you not like the way you look? Write down anything that bothers you. When you are done, go through your list. Mark the things that worry you the most. What do you spend the most time thinking about?

Next, take each thing on the list one by one. What can you do to change it? Think hard. You may want to share your list with your pastor. You may have a counselor friend. You may want to share it with your parents. It must be someone with whom you feel confident. This is a way to face up to your problems. You will feel better when you do. You may find some answers yourself.

Now we come to the most vital step. You must learn to accept yourself. You must accept what you can't change. I think you should take all those problems to the Lord. You may want to burn the paper in private. It may be your own little worship service with God. Give all your life to him. Give him your strong points and your weak ones. Give him your good points and the bad ones. Ask him to bless them. After all, he created you. He made the whole world out of nothing. He can take your life just as it is. He can make something beautiful out of it.

CHAPTER 9

Self-Esteem in Adults

We all have low self-esteem at times. What does this say about us? What will be the result?

It means that we all will be hurt by it. We need to feel that people accept us. If we don't, we won't be healthy people. We all need to have self-worth. If we don't have it, we won't show it to others. We will envy and hate each other. Some will have mental problems. Some will start to use drugs. Many will drink too much. There will be more violence. In the end, all of us will be hurt by it.

Why do so many women have low self-esteem? The problem seems worse today.

Three things now cause self-doubt among women. First, people now look down on wives and mothers. No one respects women who stay home all day. They say, "She is just a housewife." We see this message on television. We see it in the things we read. We see it in many of the ads. No one wants to be just a wife and mother. There is no glamour to it. People think the world has passed such women by.

Second, we judge women too much on beauty.
How a woman looks affects how she feels about
herself. It is hard for her to have self-worth if she
does not like her body. If she feels ugly, she will
feel she has no worth. People today think too much
about sex. Such people like women who are pretty.
But they reject those they think are ugly. A woman
who has no sex appeal can't compete with those
who do.

Third, some women today try to compete with
men. Women are smarter in some areas than men.
Yet in other areas men do better. Women who can't
compete with men are called dumb. Women feel bad
when they can't compete in these areas.

Why don't men have problems with how they look? It does not mean as much to them.

Boys care a lot about good looks. But they do
not mean as much to mature men. Their minds
mean more. Men must be smart to feel good about
themselves. For a woman, it is how she looks that
means the most. Some have made a joke about it.
They say women prefer beauty to brains. But that
is because they know men. Men can see better than
they can think!

A woman sees beauty as a value. That is because
men value a woman's beauty. And women value a man
for his intelligence. That is why men value being
smart. We value what the other sex values.

I have a friend who was married for nine years. Then her husband left her. I thought she was a good wife. She was loving and kind. Yet she is hurting. She thinks it was her fault that he left. She feels very bad now. Her self-esteem is very low. Her husband lied to her. Then he ran off with a younger girl. Why would she blame herself? It was her husband who did wrong.

I don't know. But it happens often. The partners who did no wrong often take the blame. They feel guilty. And they lose their self-esteem. The one who tries to hold the marriage together feels bad. She says, "I just wasn't good enough for him. I am no good. If I had been a good woman, he would not have left. I drove him to it. I was not a good sex partner. I didn't deserve him."

Who is wrong when a marriage goes bad? Often both did some wrong things. "It takes two to tango," as they say. Both are often to blame. But sometimes one partner will make up his or her mind to leave. Then all the blame is put on the other partner. "You did not meet my needs," he or she will say. "I had to have them met somewhere else." That way the one doing wrong can make the other feel guilty. The partner he rejects feels bad enough. Now he or she feels guilty too. The hurt person then takes all the blame. That is what happened to your friend.

Your friend should not start hating her husband. If she gets bitter, it will hurt her. If she starts to resent him, it will be like a cancer inside her. Tell her to look at the facts. She should ask, "Did I try to make the marriage work? Did I or my husband wreck it? Did he give me a fair chance? Maybe I could have given him the things he said he wanted. Would he have stayed if I had? Should I be hating myself like this?"

If someone rejects us, we are sure to feel bad. We will feel inferior. We will feel sorry for ourselves. It hurts when the one we love rejects us. She should see that she is a victim. She is not a worthless failure. Her husband failed her.

I know a woman who needs people. But she drives them away. She tries too hard to make them like her. She talks too much. And she complains a lot. She makes people run from her. She has a bad self-image. I think I could help her if she would let me. How can I tell her what she is doing? I don't want to make her feel worse.

You may help her, but you must take great care. The right to criticize must be earned. Even if you want to help, you must earn the right. You first have to show her that you respect her. Then you may be able to help her. You must show her love and kindness. When you are sure she trusts you, you may help her. You must make your motives clear.

First you must make sure you have made a friend of her. Then you might suggest a few things to her. But give them in small doses. And don't forget that you are not perfect. Someone may want to fix some of your bad points too.

I have had low self-esteem for a long time. I once went to a counselor to get help. I was very depressed at the time. He was not much help. He did nothing to build my self-worth. He was cold and aloof. I felt he was just doing a job. He didn't seem to care about me. How would you have tried to help me?

I feel bad when I hear stories like this. I know some counselors like the one you talked about. They often hurt people more than help. People often have low self-esteem along with their other problems. They need to feel love and kindness. Many counselors don't work that way. They are more concerned about the other problems.

People who hurt from low self-esteem need to be told certain truths. These may not be the exact words. But people need to face these facts. "You have suffered a lot. Life is hard. So far you have faced it all alone. From now on, let me help you bear your hurts. I am concerned about you. You deserve my respect. And I am going to give it to you. I want you to stop worrying about your problems. Tell me about them. The two of us will try to find some answers." Most depressed people feel that they are alone. You should help the person no longer feel alone. Then he can say,

"Someone cares. Someone knows what I am going
through. Someone has told me that I am going
to make it. I am not going to drown." That is what
counsel should be. That is what the Bible means by
"bear one another's burdens."

**You say we should build self-esteem in children.
I don't think that is right. The Bible says that
pride is wrong. In God's sight we are no more
than worms. How can you say we should have
self-esteem?**

Pride and self-esteem are not the same thing. I
know many think they are. Many think we should put
ourselves down. Then we won't sin by being proud.

I don't believe that. Years ago I spoke to a group in
Boston. An older woman came up to talk to me. She
asked me this same question. She said I was wrong.
She said that the Bible taught that self-esteem was pride.
She showed me a verse from the Bible. She read Psalm
22:6: "I am a worm, not a man." She said that God
wanted her to think of herself as being no better than
a worm. "I want to respect myself," she said. "But
God does not approve of pride."

I was touched by what she said. She had been a
missionary for forty years. She never married. She
said she could serve God better single. While she was
overseas, she became ill. She picked up a strange
disease. She was very tiny. She had lost a lot of weight.
I could tell she really loved God. And I knew God

must love her dearly. She had given him her whole life. Yet she did not think God cared very much for her. She would not accept that she had done a good job for him.

It is sad that she had been taught that she was no good. Many others in the world have been taught the same thing. Jesus did not leave his throne in heaven to save "worms." He gave himself for this little woman. He died for all of us. He was not afraid to call us his brothers and sisters. Jesus is now my brother. He has put me in the family of God. He has said I would live forever and ever. God has said that I am worth something. That is what I call self-esteem.

It is true. God does hate pride. He has said so in the Bible. But first we must know what the Bible means by pride.

The meaning of words can change over the years. A parent can feel pride when his child wins a race. A parent is proud of a child who gets good grades. But I don't believe God would be angry at such a parent.

I do not believe the Bible says that self-respect is wrong. Jesus told us to love our neighbors as ourselves. That means we are to have self-love. And we can't love others if we have no self-respect.

What does the Bible mean by pride? Pride is what happens when we do not follow the two basic commands of Jesus. He said we are to love God with all our heart and to love our neighbor. A proud person thinks he doesn't need anything or anyone. He thinks he doesn't need God. A proud person does not think he needs to bow before God. He does not think he needs to confess his sins. He feels he does not need to serve God. And he does not need to feel for others. That is why the Bible calls pride evil.

I think we can have the wrong kind of self-esteem. It could cause us to sin. A few years ago we called it the "me" generation. People thought only of themselves. It is wrong to think, "Me first." I have not taught that anyone should be like that. But I believe that it is right to think of ourselves as having worth before God.

CHAPTER **10**

Emotions –Love and Conflict

Do you believe that God has made just one person for each of us to marry?

No. I think it is wrong to think that way. A young man once told me about his thoughts. He woke up in the middle of the night. He had the feeling God wanted him to marry a certain girl. He had dated her only once or twice. They were not going together at the time. They did not know each other well. The next morning he called her. He told her what he thought God had said to him. The girl thought she could not argue with God. She agreed to marry him. They got married shortly after that. They have been married for seven years. They have had trouble from the very beginning.

God has given us a certain amount of free choice. He has not guaranteed us all an easy marriage. If you don't think so, you are in for a shock. This does not mean that he does not care. Marriage is a big decision. And God has promised to guide us. We should seek his will about the person we marry. I prayed many times before I proposed to my wife. We are God's children. Yet I don't think God runs a match-making service. He has given us judgment. He wants us to use our common sense. He expects us to use these in choosing a mate. If we don't believe that, we may have problems. We should not put the blame on God if things go wrong. Some might say, "If God doesn't will it, he can stop us from getting married." This is wrong.

Do you think love for a wife or husband lasts all our lives?

It can. And it should. But love is fragile. It is like a tender flower. It must be cared for and protected. If a husband works all the time, love can die. Love needs time for romance. Couples need to talk to each other. Routine can make a marriage dull. Couples need to ask themselves some questions: Where does my marriage rank in my values? Does it get the leftovers? Or does it come first? Is it worth a lot to me? Is it worth working for to make it last? Love can die if we don't tend to it.

I am a nineteen-year-old girl. I'm still single. I hear about some bad things that can happen in a marriage. If that is true, why should I bother to get married?

A bad marriage is hard, I agree. But a good marriage is a great treasure. My marriage to Shirley is the best thing that ever happened to me. There are millions who can say the same. Life has problems whether you are married or single. If you are single, you will have problems of one kind. If married, you will have other troubles. I will give you the advice I was once given: Don't marry the person you can live with. Marry the person you can't live without. If that person comes along, then marry. But you must know that marriage has its problems. It will take your best effort to make it work.

Do you think married people who are happy should never fight?

No. Good marriages are those where the couple has learned how to fight. They need to learn good ways to get rid of their anger. They should not tear each other apart. There is a good and a bad way to differ with your mate. In a bad marriage, the anger is thrown at the person. It is not thrown at the problem. Husbands may say things like, "You are dumb. You get more like your mother every day." This kind of remark *bad* strikes at the heart. It attacks the wife's self-worth. It causes a lot of problems inside for the person. It can destroy a marriage. There is a better way to approach the problem. You could say, "You are spending money faster than I can earn it." Or, "It hurts me when you don't tell me you will be late for meals." You could say, "I was embarrassed when you made me look foolish at the party last night." These remarks go after *good* the problem. These areas of struggle can be emotional and tense. The way we respond can damage a person's ego. A healthy couple should learn to work through problems without doing lasting damage.

Those who are just married need to learn how to fight fairly. If they don't, they may keep the anger inside. Then they start to resent their partner. Or they may attack the other person's ego. Either way, they are the kinds of people who fill the divorce courts.

I am sure I am losing my husband. He seems to be bored with me. He takes no interest in me. He is rude in public. He is silent at home. We have no sex life now. I have begged him to love me. But I seem to be losing ground. What can I do to save my marriage?

What you describe is what I call "the trapped feeling." I see many men who think as your husband does. He may be saying, "I am thirty-five years old. I'm not getting any younger. Do I want to spend the rest of my life with this woman? I'm bored with her. There are other women who interest me more. But there is no way out for me. I am stuck." This is what he may be thinking. These thoughts come before he starts being unfaithful. They may come when there is a strain between husband and wife.

What should a woman do when she sees these things happen? What can she do when her husband feels trapped? She could make the cage around him stronger. But that would be the worst thing she could do. That may be what she first tries to do. She sees how much he means to her. She wonders what she would ever do if he left. She starts to wonder if he is involved with other women. In fear, she tries to hold onto him. Her begging and pleading only make him respect her less. The marriage gets worse and worse.

There is a better way. She should not say, "Why do you treat me this way?" Avoid saying, "Why won't you talk to me?" Don't say, "Why don't you care anymore?" A wife should pull back herself. When she passes him in the hall, she should move by without notice. When he is silent, she should be silent. She should not be hostile or pushy. She should not explode when he does speak to her. She should answer as he speaks to her. She should remain quiet and confident. Doing this may open the door on his trap. She is no longer clamping herself to his neck like a leech. She is letting go her grip. This would make him think in a new way about her. He may wonder if he has not gone too far. He may be losing something precious to him. If that will not turn him around, then the relationship is dead.

What I suggest is hard to put in words. I am sure some will not understand what I am saying. I am saying that you should not rise up in anger. Do not stamp your feet and demand your rights as a wife. Do not sulk or pout in silence. Don't join the many women today who are coming together to wage a war against men. Nothing looks good about an angry woman grabbing for her share. The answer is not found in being hostile. The answer will come in quiet self-respect.

Keep your dignity the way you did back in your dating days. Be willing to say, "I love you. I commit myself to you. But I control only half of our marriage. I can't make you love me. You came to me of your own free will. No one forced us. The same free will is needed to keep our love alive. If you choose to walk away, I will be hurt. I have not held back any of myself. But I will let you go, and I will survive. I couldn't make you love me at the start. I can't make you now."

Sometimes this change on your part will bring a change in him.

I love my wife. And I know she loves me. But we are growing farther apart. Our relationship is stale. All we do is work. She cleans the house and cares for the kids. I fix the roof and repair the car. We do all the routine things. It is having a bad effect on our marriage. We can't seem to change our life-style. What can we do to liven up our marriage?

What you describe is what I call the "straight life." There is a lot of routine in living. It can be hard on a marriage. To go on like that is to give up something good in marriage. I suggest you try to put four elements back into your marriage. Start with pleasure. You and your wife should go on a date at least once a week. Leave the kids at home. Also take up some form of sports or pastime fun as a family.

②Second, you should try to light the fires of romance. Use love notes. Surprise her with a candlelight dinner. Take her on a sudden weekend trip.

③Third, try to reserve some time and energy for sex. Tired bodies make for tired sex. Be creative with the physical side of your marriage.

④Fourth, try to build each other up . Self-esteem needs can best be met in marriage. Nothing adds more to closeness than respect for each other.

Adults must learn to cope with the concerns of the straight life. But these duties need not wreck your mental and physical health and marriage.

I hate to admit it. But my husband cannot meet my needs. He is not romantic. He won't talk to me. I think he will always be like that. It is like our relationship is set in concrete. I want to hang on to marriage as you said I should. But I am now thinking about divorce. I don't want to do it. But I am starting to argue with myself. I can't decide if I should bail out or not. People tell me that divorce is the answer. Is it the answer for people like me?

I have seen many women go through what you describe. Many of them think about divorce. They think about it from both sides. They weigh the good side and the bad side of it.

Such a woman worries about what the divorce will do to the kids. Will she be able to support them?

Round and round she goes. She thinks about the pros and cons. Should I or shouldn't I? She is drawn to the idea. And she is repelled by it.

This is the thinking stage. It is like an old movie film. The camera catches an event of high drama. A man is on top of a tall tower. He has just built a set of wings for himself. He is trying to decide to jump or not. He is not sure the wings will work. He looks over the side. He paces back and forth. Next he stands on the rail. He is trying to get the courage to jump. "Should I, or shouldn't I? If the wings work, I'll be famous. If not, I will be killed." What a gamble!

In some ways the woman is like the man thinking of jumping. She knows that divorce can do great harm. But she wonders if she might fly away with new freedom. Does she have the courage? Will she make the jump? No, she decides to stay. On the other hand, this could be the way out. After all, others are getting a divorce. She can't decide. But often she goes ahead and jumps.

But what happens then? The wings of the ones I have seen don't open. They don't let her fly off to freedom. After the legal battle comes the custody fight. And then they argue over the house and money. Then life gets back to a boring routine. She has to get a job to keep up the home. Her skills are very few. She can be a waitress. Or she can get some office job. Or she can be a sales lady. But by the time she pays for the baby-sitter, she has little left. Her energy level

is even lower. She comes home tired to face the needs
of her kids. They irritate her. It has become a very
hard life.

Then she looks at her ex-husband. He is doing
much better. He earns more money than she. And
he has no kids to care for. And he has much more freedom. And in today's world he is better off. There is
more status in being a divorced man than a divorced
woman. He often finds another lover. She is younger
and pretty. She looks nicer than his first wife. His
former wife is jealous even more. And now she is
depressed again.

This is no made-up story. I don't tell it just to
discourage divorce. It is a very common pattern.
Many women get a divorce for these same reasons
(as opposed to unfaithfulness). Most live to regret
the divorce. Later she may see the good qualities of her
husband. He now looks good to her. But she bailed out.
It is too late then.

Divorce is not the answer. Busy husbands and
lonely wives need a better answer than that. Just
because others are doing it doesn't mean you should.
The world takes marriage very lightly now. Divorce
is more and more common. But the Bible has not
changed. The book of Malachi tells what God thinks
of divorce. It says that God no longer heard the
people's prayers. The reason was "because the Lord
has seen your evil in divorcing your wives. . . . When
you married, the two of you became one person in

God's sight. And what does he want? Godly children from your union. So guard your passions! Keep faith with the wife of your youth. For the Lord, the God of Israel, hates divorce" (Malachi 2:14-16).

I think I see a blind spot in my life. It is in the way I think about my wife. I thought I had done my job if I met my family's need for money. And I knew I should be faithful to my wife. I thought that was enough. Do you say I am responsible to help meet her emotional needs, too?

That is right. Women today are under attack by the world. All that they have been taught is now being laughed at. Every day some of our Christian values are being mocked and torn down. Some of these are:

1. The idea that being a mother is worth a woman's time is being challenged. People think that a woman should find a life outside the home.
2. The idea that man and wife become one flesh at marriage is not accepted now. They don't like the thought that they must find their identity in each other. People want to be individuals. They want to compete rather than be one. Some women believe being one with a man is an insult.
3. People no longer believe that divorce is wrong. Most people have given up on the idea of a lifetime marriage.

4. The ideal woman mentioned in Proverbs 31 is no longer thought of as an ideal.
5. Women no longer like the idea of being helpmates. They look down on being the one who bakes the bread. They don't want to patch wounds, give love, build homes, or bear children. To them, these things are disgusting.

All of these old values are passing away. Women who try to keep them are under attack. It is like the wrath of hell coming down on them. The television and all the other media are teaching other values. They are trying to tear down all the Christian values. It is hard to hang on to them. Women who want to live up to them are called stupid and old-fashioned. Their self-esteem suffers because of it. They are fighting against a big movement. And they get very little support from others.

It is time for men to stand with their wives. They should be happy for wives who want to hang onto these values. Such a wife stays at home all day with jelly-faced toddlers. She copes with strong-willed teenagers. It is time she gets her husband's emotional support. That means more than washing the dishes and sweeping the floor. I mean emotional support. He should talk to her and make her feel like a lady. He should build up her ego. She needs a day to relax each week. He should take her out to dinner. Most of all, he should tell her he loves her. Without these, she has no

defense. She stands alone against the enemies of the
family. They are also the enemies of his family!

What effect do these ways of thinking have on marriage?

It can do a lot of harm. If a woman has no emotional
support, it puts a great strain on the marriage. The man
becomes the only person with whom she can talk. She
has no other place to vent her feelings. She has no
other friendships. And he is her only source of love.
But she is not the only concern he has. He has his own
pressures on the job. His business takes all his time.
His self-esteem hangs on how well he does his job.
And the whole family depends on what he earns. By
the time he gets home, he is tired and empty. And he
may not really understand his wife. He does not know
what she needs. He does not know how lonely she is.
And by that time, he has very little strength left to
prop her up.

A wife needs to know certain things about her
husband. He is very busy and does not always talk to
his wife. A wife cannot depend on such a man to meet
all her needs. She will always be frustrated by his
failure. Instead, if you are a woman, you must find
some women friends. You need to talk with them.
Learn to laugh, gripe, dream, and have fun with them.
There are many wives around you who are just like
you. They will be looking for you as you begin to look
for them. Get into an exercise class. Find some hobby

groups. Look for a church or Bible study group. Join a bicycle club or some other group. But, by all means, don't sit in your four walls all the time. Don't sit around feeling sorry for yourself as you wait for your man to come home on his white horse.

FINAL WORD

I wrote this book to give help you could use. I also
wanted to write it in a form you could use. I thought
questions and answers would help. I want to say again
why I thought this book was needed. I also want to
state the beliefs that lie behind my answers.

Years ago when a baby was born, the new mother
had friends around her. They came to give her help
and advice. Aunts, grandmothers, and friends came.
None of them had ever read a book about raising kids.
But they knew how. They brought a certain kind of
folk wisdom. They felt sure about how we were to
raise kids. They had an answer for almost any problem.
It may not have been right. But they had answers. In
that way, the new mother was taught how to "mother."
Older mothers taught her.

But this help is gone today. Parents live too far
away. The job of being a mother scares young wives.
We move around a lot. The people next door are often
strangers to us. Parents may live miles away. So young
parents have a lot of fears. They know very little about
raising a family. Dr. Benjamin Spock talked about
young mothers he knew. They cried the morning they

took their new babies home. "I won't know what to do," they would say.

Such fear sends parents running to experts. They want help and advice. They look to doctors, counselors, and teachers. Many raise their kids just as the "experts" tell them. In this country, we turn to paid experts for help. We do so more than any other country.

Have these experts helped us? Our kids should be better than in other years. But it is not true. More kids now turn to drugs and alcohol. More girls are getting pregnant. There is more mental illness. There is more suicide among teens. In many ways we have been very bad parents. I don't blame all this on the experts. But I think they helped make the mess. Why? Because most have not based their work on the Bible. They have set aside God's wisdom. They have thrown away the ethics that we used to build on.

These experts turn to their own ideas. Each writes from his own viewpoint. They show their own bias. They don't believe in God. But they think they can play God. And they turn others away from him. They ignore the Bible's wisdom. They give instead their own silly opinions. Parents are in bad need of help. So they turn to these "experts." They have nowhere else to go. I talked to a young mother. She worked with a youth project. A psychologist came to help them. He was to teach a class for young girls. The class was to give the girls a healthy feeling about sex. The counselor gave them his beliefs. He said girls, when they are twelve years old, should have sex with their fathers. That would give them a healthy view of sex. That may shock you. It shocked me, too. Yet this is where morals today have gone. Many of the "experts" do not believe in standard values. They say morals are a matter of one's own beliefs.

I have tried to give reasons for my answers. How do they differ from the other "experts"? They differ because of the source of these views. My views come from the Bible. God gave us principles to live by. We have had them all through the years. We are to teach them to our kids. But now the experts tell us these things are not true.

I wrote this book to give what I think is the Bible's view. What is my view? I think parents are to control their kids with love and care. Kids need to learn self-control. Parents need to seek the best for their kids. Each member of the family must respect the others. Parents must be faithful to each other. The family must hold to God's standards. I could boil them down to four statements. They are these:

1. I believe all human life has worth. The unborn and the old have value. The widows and those who have mental illness are loved by God. Life begins when we are conceived. It continues to the grave. All have worth.
2. I believe in marriage. It should last all of life. Even in sickness or trouble, we should hold to marriage.

3. I believe we should commit ourselves to the task of being parents. The world is in a mess. It makes this job hard. But being a parent demands our best.
4. I believe we must make sure we have eternal life in Christ. We must share this life with our family and with the world. We must commit ourselves and our families to this end. No other effort should concern us more.

All of these standards are under attack today. Yet these views will work for us. As long as we have parents and kids, we will need them. Nothing can take their place.

WORD FREQUENCY LIST
(List does not include some proper names)

a 520
able 10
about 133
abuse 2
abused 1
accept 19
acceptance 1
accepted 2
acne 1
across 2
act 7
acted 2
action 1
actions 1
acts 5
Adam 1
add 1
added 1
adds 2
admit 2
adolescence 1
adolescent 1
adopt 1
adopted 3
ads 2
adult 5
adults 11
advice 3
affect 5
affected 1
affects 2
afford 1
afraid 12
after 15
again 13
against 6
age 31
aged 1
agents 1
ages 2

ago 10
agree 9
agreed 1
ahead 2
air 1
alcohol 1
alive 1
all 104
allow 1
allowed 2
almost 1
alone 10
along 4
aloof 1
also 23
always 6
am 35
among 2
amount 1
an 22
and 292
anger 11
angry 28
animal 1
Ann 4
another 7
another's 1
answer 18
answers 8
any 20
anybody 1
anymore 2
anyone 4
anything 8
anyway 2
apart 2
appeal 1
appear 1
appetites 1
approach 2

approve 1
are 239
areas 4
argue 5
arguing 1
arm 1
arms 2
around 21
arrested 1
arrived 1
art 1
as 83
ashamed 1
aside 1
ask 19
asked 7
asking 1
asks 1
assure 1
at 111
attack 7
attacked 1
attacks 1
attitudes 1
aunts 1
authority 1
avoid 3
awake 1
aware 1
away 30
babies 3
baby 10
baby-sitter 1
back 23
backyard 1
bad 42
badge 1
badly 4
bail 1
bailed 1

bakes 1
balance 1
ball 1
bang 2
base 2
based 2
basic 1
basis 1
basketball 1
bathe 1
battle 4
be 242
beans 3
bear 3
beat 1
beautiful 1
beauty 5
became 3
because 27
become 4
becomes 5
bed 7
bed-wetting 1
been 34
before 22
beg 1
began 10
begged 1
begging 1
begin 8
beginning 1
begins 3
begs 2
behalf 1
behave 6
behavior 6
behind 3
being 36
belief 1
beliefs 7

believe 27
believes 3
belong 1
belt 1
bend 1
Benjamin 1
best 18
better 27
between 6
bias 1
Bible 26
Bible's 2
bicycle 1
big 9
bike 1
bill 1
Billie 1
bills 1
birth 1
bite 1
bitter 1
black 1
blackheads 1
blame 9
blamed 1
bleachers 1
bless 1
blind 1
block 4
blocked 1
blow 1
bluff 1
blush 1
boat 3
bodies 6
body 6
boil 1
boiling 1
bomb 1
book 8

books 3	calls 1	Christ 1	controlled 2	date 5
boots 1	calm 2	Christian 5	convinced 1	dated 1
borders 3	came 15	Christians 3	cook 1	dates 1
bored 2	camera 1	church 12	cope 2	dating 4
boring 2	camping 1	claim 1	copes 1	daughter 12
born 5	can 131	clamping 1	corner 1	daughter's 1
boss 5	can't 35	class 14	could 49	daughters 2
Boston 1	cancer 1	classroom 1	couldn't 3	David 2
both 14	candlelight 1	clean 3	counsel 1	day 30
bother 1	candy 4	cleans 1	counselor 3	days 8
bothering 1	cannot 3	clear 8	counselors 3	dead 2
bothers 1	car 12	clench 1	count 2	deal 5
bottom 2	cards 1	climb 2	country 5	deals 1
bought 3	care 20	clocks 1	counts 1	dearly 1
bow 1	cared 2	close 3	couple 3	death 2
boy 25	careful 4	closely 1	couples 2	debate 1
boy-girl 1	careless 1	closeness 2	courage 9	decide 6
boy-type 1	cares 3	closer 1	court 1	decided 1
boys 22	carrot 1	clothes 8	courteous 1	decides 1
brace 1	carry 2	cloud 1	courts 1	decision 1
brains 2	cars 1	club 1	cousin 1	deep 1
brat 1	case 1	clumped 1	cousin's 1	defend 1
bread 1	cases 1	cold 2	cover 2	defense 2
break 7	castles 3	collar 2	cowboys 1	deformed 2
breakfast 1	catch 1	collects 1	coyote 3	defy 1
breaking 2	catches 1	college 1	coyotes 2	demand 4
breaks 1	caught 1	color 1	crawl 2	demands 1
breasts 2	cause 9	combat 2	crawled 3	democracy 1
breath 1	caused 4	come 38	crazy 1	dentist 12
bridge 3	causes 7	comes 20	created 1	dentist's 2
brightly 1	causing 1	comforted 1	creative 1	depend 3
bring 3	certain 7	coming 8	cried 2	depends 4
broad 1	chair 8	command 4	cries 8	depressed 4
broke 1	challenge 4	commands 1	critical 1	describe 3
broken 1	challenged 2	commit 3	criticize 2	deserve 3
brother 2	chance 2	common 5	cross 1	deserved 1
brothers 2	change 16	compare 2	crucial 1	desires 1
brought 1	changed 1	compared 1	cruel 1	despise 1
brownie 1	changes 12	comparing 1	crummy 1	destroy 3
build 10	charge 2	compete 6	crushed 1	diaper 5
building 2	cheek 1	complains 2	cry 8	did 56
built 2	chew 1	conceived 1	crying 6	didn't 15
burdens 1	chief 1	concern 3	crystal 1	die 4
burn 1	child 185	concerned 2	culture 1	died 1
burned 1	child's 14	concerns 1	curse 1	differ 3
burst 1	childhood 1	concrete 1	curved 1	dignified 1
bus 3	childish 1	confess 1	custody 1	dignity 6
business 2	children 74	confidence 2	cut 1	dinner 4
busy 4	children's 1	confident 3	cycle 1	dirt 1
but 173	China 1	conflict 1	dad 4	discipline 16
buy 2	choice 3	conflicts 1	daddies 1	disciplining 2
by 62	choices 3	confuse 1	daddy 2	discourage 1
cage 2	choose 5	cons 1	daily 1	disease 2
call 9	chooses 1	contest 1	damage 6	disgusting 1
called 10	choosing 1	continues 1	damaged 1	dishes 1
calling 1	chores 1	control 26	dark 1	dislike 1

Disneyland 1
disobeys 2
divorce 15
divorced 3
divorcing 1
do 206
doctor 6
doctors 3
does 66
doesn't 13
dog 3
dogs 1
doing 26
don't 142
done 12
door 5
doors 2
doorway 1
doses 1
double 1
doubt 2
doubts 3
down 26
drama 1
draw 1
drawn 1
dream 2
drink 3
drive 2
driver 1
driver's 1
drivers 1
drives 2
driving 1
dropping 1
drops 1
drove 4
drown 3
drown 1
drowned 1
drugs 3
dry 3
dull 2
dumb 5
dump 1
during 14
duties 1
each 42
ear 1
early 7
earn 5
earned 1
earns 2
ears 4
ease 1
easy 15

eat 17
eating 2
eats 1
edge 2
effect 4
effects 1
effort 2
efforts 1
egg 1
ego 6
eight 3
eighteen 1
eighth 1
eighty 1
either 7
electric 2
elements 1
elevator 1
Eli 3
Eli's 1
else 10
embarrass 1
embarrassed 1
emotion 1
emotional 10
emotions 2
empty 3
encourage 2
end 7
enemies 2
energy 3
enforce 2
England 1
enjoy 5
enjoyed 3
enough 10
enters 1
envy 1
equal 1
esteem 1
eternal 1
ethics 1
Eve 1
even 27
evening 1
event 1
ever 15
every 8
everyone 1
evil 3
ex-husband 1
exact 2
example 2
examples 1
excite 1
excited 1

exercise 1
expect 10
expecting 1
expects 3
expert 1
experts 10
explain 2
explained 1
explode 1
explore 2
exposed 1
eye 1
eyes 2
face 13
faced 1
faces 1
fact 5
facts 2
fail 1
failed 1
fails 1
failure 4
failures 1
faint 1
fair 6
fairly 1
faith 1
faithful 2
falls 1
families 3
family 24
family's 1
famous 1
far 6
farther 1
fast 1
faster 2
fastest 1
father 15
fathers 4
fault 3
fear 4
fears 3
feed 3
feeding 1
feel 66
feeling 11
feelings 18
feels 16
feet 3
fell 1
felt 9
fence 3
fenders 2
few 19
fewer 1

fifteen 5
fifth 2
fight 11
fighting 3
fill 1
filled 4
film 1
films 1
final 1
find 20
finds 1
fine 2
finger 3
fingers 1
finished 1
fired 1
fires 2
firm 8
first 45
fishing 1
fists 1
fit 1
five 7
fix 2
fixed 2
flashing 1
flesh 1
flew 1
flipped 1
floor 9
flower 1
fly 2
flying 2
folk 1
follow 2
followed 1
food 5
foods 1
foolish 2
foot 2
for 175
force 3
forced 3
foreign 1
forests 1
forever 1
forget 5
forgive 2
fork 1
form 4
former 1
forth 1
forty 1
forward 1
fought 1
found 4

foundation 1
four 12
four-year-old 1
fourteen 8
fourth 6
fragile 2
Fred 3
free 10
freedom 8
freely 1
fresh 1
friend 12
friends 17
friendships 1
frighten 1
Frisbees 1
from 53
front 2
fruit 2
frustrate 1
frustrated 1
fun 14
funny 3
fuse 1
fussing 1
fussy 2
future 2
gain 1
gamble 1
game 10
games 4
gap 1
garage 1
gas 1
gave 9
generation 2
gentle 4
get 67
gets 18
getting 5
girl 14
girl's 1
girls 13
give 36
given 9
giver 1
gives 2
glad 1
glamour 1
go 43
goal 1
God 77
God's 8
godly 1
goes 5
going 26

gone 5	hangs 1	hole 1	insult 3	kind 23
good 52	happen 7	holes 1	intelligence 1	kindness 2
good-looking 1	happened 5	holy 1	intend 1	kinds 5
goodness 1	happening 2	home 38	interest 2	kitchen 1
got 8	happens 7	homely 1	into 14	knew 19
gotten 1	happy 7	homes 5	introduction 1	knobs 1
grabbing 1	hard 40	honest 2	invite 3	knock 2
grade 2	harder 6	honor 2	invited 1	know 115
graders 1	hardest 2	hope 2	involved 3	knowing 1
grades 2	harm 10	hopeless 1	iron 1	knows 19
grandmothers 1	harms 2	hormones 1	ironed 1	lacks 1
grandparent 1	harsh 3	horse 1	irritate 1	lady 2
grave 1	has 69	hostile 3	is 446	land 2
gravity 1	hassle 1	hot 2	isn't 1	lands 1
greasy 1	hate 10	hour 1	Israel 1	lap 1
great 6	hateful 1	hours 1	it 373	larger 1
grew 1	hates 3	house 8	item 1	last 20
grinned 1	hating 3	houses 1	items 1	lasting 1
grip 1	haul 1	housewife 1	its 2	lasts 1
gripe 1	haunt 1	how 106	jealous 2	late 9
grocery 1	have 234	human 4	jeep 2	later 22
grouchy 1	haven't 2	humans 1	jeeps 1	laugh 10
ground 2	having 6	humor 1	jelly-faced 1	laughed 7
grounds 1	Hazel 5	hundreds 2	jerk 1	laughing 2
group 7	he 499	hungry 3	Jesus 6	law 3
groups 4	he's 2	hurt 30	Joan 8	lay 1
grow 15	heads 1	hurting 2	job 17	lazy 2
growing 10	health 4	hurts 15	jobs 4	lead 4
grown 5	healthy 9	husband 19	Joe 1	leader 2
grows 8	hear 6	husband's 1	John 1	leaders 2
growth 1	heard 9	husbands 2	join 2	leaking 1
gruff 1	hearing 1	I 518	joke 1	leaky 1
grumpy 3	hears 2	I'd 1	jokes 1	learn 48
guaranteed 1	heart 3	I'll 2	joyful 1	learned 6
guard 1	heaven 1	I'm 7	judge 3	learning 1
guest 1	heavy 1	I've 1	judgment 1	learns 4
guests 1	held 2	idea 9	juice 1	least 4
guide 3	hell 1	ideal 2	jump 4	leave 12
guided 1	help 77	ideas 1	jumped 1	leaving 1
guilt 1	help-mates 1	identity 1	jumping 1	led 3
guilty 6	helped 5	if 136	jumps 1	leech 1
gum 2	helps 2	ignore 1	junior 5	left 8
gun 1	her 155	ignored 1	junk 1	leftovers 1
guns 1	here 4	ill 1	just 36	leg 1
gym 1	heroes 1	illness 2	justice 3	legal 1
had 55	herself 5	important 10	keep 17	legs 1
hair 1	hide 2	improve 2	keeping 1	less 3
half 2	high 7	in 214	keeps 2	lesson 1
hall 3	him 185	in-between 1	kept 1	let 43
hand 4	himself 17	includes 1	key 4	let's 1
handicap 1	his 147	Indians 1	keys 1	letdown 1
handicapped 1	hit 12	individuals 1	kid 6	lets 1
handle 2	hits 1	inferior 5	kids 130	letter 1
handled 1	hitting 1	inside 3	killed 2	letters 1
hands 4	hobby 1	insist 1	killing 3	letting 1
hang 5	hold 10	instead 3	killings 1	level 1

license 1	made 19	mind 5	neither 1	opens 1
lie 2	made-up 1	minds 3	never 18	opinions 1
lied 1	major 1	minority 1	new 12	opposed 1
life 39	make 86	minute 1	next 11	or 91
life-style 1	makes 11	minutes 2	nice 6	order 2
lifetime 2	making 6	miss 1	nicely 1	ordered 1
light 1	Malachi 2	missed 1	nicer 1	Oregon 1
lightly 1	male 1	misses 1	night 12	organs 1
lights 2	man 19	missionary 1	night's 1	orphans 1
like 72	many 53	mistake 6	nine 3	other 78
liked 1	mark 1	mistakes 3	nineteen 2	others 55
likely 1	marked 1	mistreat 1	no 78	our 47
likes 2	marriage 33	mixed 1	noise 1	ourselves 7
liking 1	marriages 1	mocked 1	none 1	out 42
limits 11	married 11	models 1	nor 1	outside 5
line 4	marries 2	moist 1	normal 1	over 26
list 5	marry 8	molded 1	north 1	overseas 1
listen 10	Mary 4	mom 2	not 272	overweight 2
little 23	master 1	moments 1	notebook 1	own 29
live 14	match-making 1	money 15	notes 1	paces 1
lived 1	mate 2	month 1	nothing 14	paid 1
liven 1	matter 5	months 8	notice 3	pain 3
lives 5	mature 5	morals 3	noticed 1	painful 1
living 1	may 115	more 63	now 51	paint 1
load 1	maybe 5	morning 8	number 1	pair 1
locked 1	me 101	most 32	nursery 1	panic 1
lonely 2	meal 2	mostly 1	o'clock 1	paper 1
long 14	meals 2	mother 44	obey 18	parent 41
longer 9	mean 25	mothers 5	obeyed 1	parent's 2
look 35	meaning 2	motives 1	obeying 1	parenting 3
looked 5	means 13	motto 1	obeys 1	parents 114
looking 4	meant 3	mountains 1	object 1	parking 2
looks 12	measures 1	mouth 1	objective 1	parks 1
loose 2	meat 1	move 3	occur 1	part 11
lord 5	meddler 1	movement 1	of 297	parties 1
lose 5	media 1	movie 1	off 16	partner 5
loses 4	meet 8	movies 1	offer 1	partners 1
losing 5	meeting 1	mow 1	office 6	party 2
loss 1	meetings 1	much 41	often 28	passed 1
lost 2	meets 1	music 3	oil 5	passes 1
lot 33	member 1	must 99	ok 1	passing 1
lots 2	men 17	my 119	old 42	passions 1
loud 1	menstrual 1	myself 7	old-fashioned 1	past 2
louder 3	mental 7	name 1	older 9	pastime 1
love 77	mentally 1	named 1	on 123	pastor 2
loved 13	mentioned 1	narrow 1	once 15	patch 1
lovely 2	mercy 1	naturally 1	one 78	patient 2
lover 2	mess 2	near 4	one's 2	patients 1
loves 6	message 2	nearly 4	oneness 1	patrol 1
loving 6	met 3	neat 1	ones 6	pattern 1
low 8	middle 5	neck 1	only 14	pay 7
lower 1	might 12	need 64	onto 4	paying 1
lowers 2	mild 1	needed 3	open 6	pays 2
lunch 1	mile 1	needs 41	opened 1	peace 1
lungs 1	miles 2	neighbor 2	opener 1	peaceful 1
mad 1	millions 1	neighbors 1	openly 1	peers 1

penis 1	pressures 2	raise 5	rest 7	scary 1
pens 1	pretty 2	raised 2	restaurant 1	schedule 1
people 63	price 1	raising 3	result 3	school 16
people's 2	priceless 1	ran 3	return 2	schoolbooks 1
percent 1	pride 10	rank 1	reward 2	schoolwork 2
perfect 4	principles 1	rate 3	rewarded 1	scold 1
period 1	private 1	rather 2	rich 1	scout 1
permissive 1	privileges 1	rational 1	rid 2	scratch 1
person 26	problem 15	rats 4	ridicule 1	scream 3
person's 3	problems 41	reach 5	right 36	screamed 1
pet 1	process 1	reached 1	rights 1	seat 1
pets 2	project 1	reaches 1	rigid 1	second 9
physical 2	promise 3	reacts 1	rise 1	secret 1
pick 5	promised 2	read 6	risk 1	secrets 1
picked 2	pronounce 1	reading 3	river 1	secure 7
picks 1	prop 1	ready 12	road 1	see 35
picture 1	proposed 1	real 3	Robert 6	seek 3
piece 2	pros 1	really 10	Robert's 1	seem 8
pieces 2	protect 4	reason 6	rock 4	seems 5
pilot 2	protected 1	reasons 5	rode 1	seen 7
pimples 3	protein 1	rebel 4	rogue 1	sees 3
pin 2	proud 5	rebels 1	role 2	self 1
pins 3	prove 4	record 1	romance 3	self-concept 1
place 13	proverb 2	records 1	romantic 1	self-confidence 2
placed 1	Proverbs 1	red 1	roof 3	self-control 4
places 1	Psalm 1	refers 2	room 4	self-defense 1
plan 7	psychologist 1	refused 2	roots 2	self-disciplined 1
plane 3	puberty 1	regret 1	rosy 1	self-doubt 3
play 10	public 3	reject 2	rotten 1	self-doubts 1
played 5	pull 1	rejected 1	rough 1	self-esteem 29
player 1	pulled 2	rejection 1	round 2	self-image 1
playing 1	punish 24	rejects 3	routine 4	self-love 1
plays 1	punished 8	relate 1	rude 2	self-respect 5
pleading 1	punishment 3	relates 1	ruin 1	self-worth 8
pleasure 2	pup 1	relations 1	rule 4	selfish 3
pledge 1	pure 1	relationship 3	rules 12	send 2
plug 1	purpose 9	relax 1	run 7	sending 1
point 2	pushy 1	relieved 1	running 1	sends 1
pointed 2	put 23	rely 1	runs 4	sense 4
points 3	puts 1	remain 3	runway 4	sensitive 1
police 4	putting 1	remark 1	sad 3	serious 1
policeman 3	qualities 1	remarks 1	safe 4	serve 2
poor 3	question 10	remember 7	safety 1	service 2
poorly 2	questions 5	remembers 1	said 61	set 7
popular 1	quicker 1	remind 1	sales 1	seven 8
pores 2	quickly 1	reminded 1	same 37	seventeen 4
potty-trained 1	quiet 6	repair 2	sarcastic 1	seventh 1
pout 3	quietly 1	repelled 1	sass 1	several 1
power 1	quit 1	required 1	save 3	sex 13
pray 2	race 1	resent 2	saved 1	sexes 1
prayed 1	radio 1	reserve 1	saw 6	sexual 1
prayers 1	raft 1	respect 42	Sawyer 1	shall 1
precious 2	rafts 1	respects 3	say 78	shamed 2
prefers 1	rail 1	respond 4	saying 6	shape 2
pregnant 1	rails 2	responsibility 1	says 16	shaping 1
pressure 2	rain 2	responsible 4	scares 1	share 6

she 231	sleep 1	stand 5	suffer 2	temper 2
she'll 1	slipping 1	standards 2	suffered 1	ten 6
shed 2	slow 1	stands 2	suffers 2	ten-year-old 1
shined 1	slowly 1	start 20	sugar 2	tend 2
ship 1	smacked 1	started 1	suggest 5	tender 4
Shirley 1	small 9	starting 2	suicide 1	tense 2
shirt 1	smart 2	starts 5	suit 1	test 2
shirts 1	smarter 3	state 1	sulk 1	testing 1
shock 4	smashed 1	statement 1	Sunday 2	tests 1
shocked 4	smell 1	statements 1	superman 1	than 34
shocks 1	smooth 1	status 1	support 7	thank 2
shoes 1	so 33	stay 10	supposed 3	thanked 1
shook 1	social 5	stayed 1	sure 20	that 310
shooting 2	socked 1	stays 2	surprise 1	the 898
shops 1	soft 2	steady 1	surprised 1	their 107
short 2	softly 2	steals 1	survive 1	them 204
shortly 1	solve 6	steel 2	Suzie 1	themselves 15
should 186	some 95	steer 2	sweeping 1	then 81
shouldn't 3	someday 2	step 5	switch 1	there 56
show 24	someone 13	stepped 1	system 2	therefore 1
showed 6	something 19	steps 3	table 4	these 93
showing 3	sometimes 5	stick 6	take 43	they 406
shown 1	somewhere 3	still 13	taken 1	thing 21
shows 4	son 24	stings 1	takes 11	things 100
shy 5	son's 1	stop 8	taking 5	think 129
sick 1	songs 1	stopped 3	talk 31	thinking 10
sickness 2	sons 5	stops 1	talked 6	thinks 8
side 6	soon 8	store 4	talking 1	third 5
sides 1	sooner 2	stories 1	talks 1	thirteen 3
sight 3	soothing 1	story 3	tall 1	thirty-five 1
sign 1	sorrow 1	stove 1	tame 1	this 114
signs 1	sorry 9	stoves 1	tango 1	those 23
silence 1	sorts 1	straight 2	tantrum 1	thought 22
silent 3	sounds 1	strain 3	task 2	thoughtful 1
silly 6	source 2	strange 3	tasks 1	thoughtless 1
simple 2	spank 20	strange-looking 1	taste 3	thoughts 3
sin 4	spanked 4	strangers 1	taught 23	thousand 1
since 1	spanking 21	strayed 1	teach 26	three 11
single 6	speak 3	strength 6	teacher 17	throats 1
sins 1	speaks 1	strengths 3	teachers 9	throne 1
sisters 5	special 1	strikes 1	teaches 1	through 22
sit 11	spend 8	strong 12	teaching 7	throw 2
sits 1	spending 1	strong-willed 1	teams 1	thrown 3
sitting 1	spent 3	stronger 2	tear 3	throws 1
six 6	spice 1	struggle 1	tears 6	thumping 1
sixteen 3	spirit 9	struggles 1	teasing 1	thy 2
sixth 2	spiritual 3	stubbed 1	teen 4	thyself 1
sixty 1	spoiled 1	stubborn 1	teenage 1	ticket 1
size 4	spoke 1	stuck 3	teenager 3	tickets 1
skiing 1	sports 3	student 1	teenagers 3	tied 1
skills 3	spot 1	students 5	teens 5	Tim 1
skin 7	squirming 1	study 2	teeth 1	time 83
slam 1	staff 1	stupid 2	television 7	times 25
slap 2	stage 2	succeed 1	tell 54	tiny 1
slapped 1	stale 1	such 15	telling 1	tired 11
slaps 2	stamp 2	sudden 1	tells 3	to 910

today 19
today's 1
toddler 2
toddlers 2
toe 1
together 8
told 24
Tom 1
tone 1
tonight 3
too 43
took 13
tools 1
tooth 2
top 2
torn 1
toss 1
total 1
touch 6
touched 2
touches 1
touching 1
tough 2
toughest 1
toward 1
tower 1
toy 1
toys 2
traced 1
train 2
trained 1
training 1
traits 1
trap 1
trapped 2
trash 1
treachery 1
treasure 1
treat 7
treated 2
tree 3
trees 2
trials 1
tried 8
tries 3
trip 2
trips 1
troop 1
trouble 12
true 20
trumpet 1
trusts 2
truths 4

try 41
trying 8
tune 1
turn 12
turned 5
turning 1
tussle 2
twelve 6
twenties 1
twenty 2
twenty-one 1
twice 1
two 22
tyrant 1
ugly 8
unborn 1
under 9
underdogs 1
undershirt 1
understand 8
unfaithful 1
unfaithfulness 1
uniform 2
union 1
unkind 3
unless 3
unruly 1
until 4
unto 2
up 73
upset 2
urges 1
us 57
use 19
used 6
using 1
vacation 1
vacations 1
Valentine's 1
valentines 1
value 9
values 12
vent 1
verse 1
verses 1
very 57
vicious 1
victim 1
view 4
viewpoint 1
views 6
violence 2
violent 1

visits 1
vital 2
voice 3
wage 1
wages 1
wait 5
waited 1
waiting 1
waitress 1
wake 1
walk 2
walked 3
walks 1
wall 1
wallet 1
walls 1
wander 1
want 102
wanted 14
wants 16
war 2
warden 1
warm 1
warmth 2
warned 2
was 136
washing 1
wasn't 4
waste 2
wasted 1
watch 7
watching 2
water 4
wave 1
waxed 1
waxing 1
way 74
ways 7
we 198
weak 10
weaker 1
weakness 3
weapon 1
wear 2
wears 1
week 4
weekend 1
weekends 1
weeks 2
weigh 1
weight 2
well 21
well-known 1

went 6
were 33
wet 2
wets 1
wetting 1
what 183
what's 1
when 115
where 18
whether 1
which 4
while 3
white 1
who 73
whole 7
whom 2
why 43
widows 2
wife 26
wife's 1
wiggle 1
wiggled 1
wiggling 1
wild 3
will 240
willful 2
willing 1
win 4
wind 1
winds 1
wings 4
wins 4
wisdom 3
wise 4
wish 1
with 147
withered 1
without 12
wives 7
woke 1
wolves 2
woman 22
woman's 2
women 23
won 1
won't 47
wonder 4
wondered 1
wonders 3
word 6
words 7
work 24
worked 2

working 1
works 5
world 18
worlds 1
worm 2
worms 2
worried 2
worry 9
worrying 1
worse 13
worship 2
worst 5
worth 14
worthless 1
worthwhile 1
worthy 1
would 89
wouldn't 1
wound 1
wounds 1
wrath 2
wreck 2
wrecked 1
wrecks 1
wristwatch 1
write 8
writes 1
written 1
wrong 36
wrote 2
yard 3
yeah 1
year 13
years 75
yell 1
yelled 1
yes 8
yet 19
yield 1
you 540
you're 1
young 25
younger 8
your 141
yours 2
yourself 10
youth 2
zone 1
zoo 2

MOR